The Field Researcher's Handbook

Related Titles from Georgetown University Press

Career Diplomacy: Life and Work in the US Foreign Service,
Second Edition
BY HARRY W. KOPP AND CHARLES K. GILLESPIE

Careers in International Affairs: Ninth Edition
EDITED BY LAURA E. CRESSEY, BARRETT J. HELMER, AND
JENNIFER E. STEFFENSEN

Working World: Careers in International Education, Exchange,
and Development, Second Edition
BY SHERRY LEE MUELLER AND MARK OVERMANN

The Field Researcher's Handbook

A Guide to the Art and Science of Professional Fieldwork

DAVID J. DANELO

Georgetown University Press | Washington, DC

Library of Congress Cataloging-in-Publication Data

Names: Danelo, David J., author.
Title: The field researcher's handbook : a guide to the art and
    science of professional fieldwork / by David J. Danelo.
Description: Washington D.C. : Georgetown University Press,
    2017. | Includes bibliographical references and index.
Identifiers: LCCN 2016033267 (print) | LCCN 2016040148
    (ebook) | ISBN 9781626164376 (pb : alk. paper) | ISBN
    9781626164451 (hc : alk. paper) | ISBN 9781626164383 (eb)
Subjects: LCSH: Social sciences—Fieldwork. | Social sciences—
    Research. | Anthropology—Fieldwork. | Research—Hand-
    books, manuals, etc. | Research—Methodology.
Classification: LCC H62 .D226 2017 (print) | LCC H62 (ebook) |
    DDC 300.72/3—dc23
LC record available at https://lccn.loc.gov/2016033267

♾ This book is printed on acid-free paper meeting the requirements of the American National Standard for Permanence in
Paper for Printed Library Materials.

18 17   9 8 7 6 5 4 3 2 First printing

Printed in the United States of America

Cover design by Faceout Studio, Charles Brock. Cover image by
Thinkstock.

for Dana and Sina

Contents

Introduction
What Is Field Research?

Have you ever traveled for the specific purpose of learning something? Taken a pilgrimage to an ancestral homeland to understand your family heritage? Gone out to a job site to find the facts from the factory instead of the conference room? Stood on a street corner and halted pedestrians to ask survey questions? Interviewed a colleague to learn a different linguistic and cultural approach to a puzzling problem? Crossed an ocean for work, study, or personal exploration?

That is field research.

Wait. Hang on a minute. Is that really all there is to it? Doesn't field research require conformity to scientific methods? Can you really call yourself a "researcher" if an Institutional Review Board, senior officer, program supervisor, or dissertation committee chair hasn't signed off on a proposal? Don't you have to be certified by a guild or government agency to be able to claim the title of field researcher?

Not at all.

Scientists, anthropologists, and sociologists define field research as "the collection of information outside a laboratory, library, or workplace setting."[1] Volumes of methodological texts weigh in with competing theories on how to process statistics and surveys, the types and styles of data collection, and reminders to keep reflexivity and positionality in mind when conducting qualitative analysis. There is a convention—especially in academic circles—to understanding the processes and particulars of what comprises field research.

But I'm not here to talk about how to understand, explain, or theorize field research. *This book is about how to do it.* Regardless of whether the context is policy analysis, data gathering, or professional investigation, fieldwork requires the ability to find relevant facts and the capacity to evaluate personal risk. In academic studies, corporate finance analyses, public policy assessments, and private client reports, researching away from home includes cultural observations, expert interviews, and data collection to analyze information and determine options.

Is there anything that can prepare us for this experience other than just doing it?

Yes, I think so.

I say this because I've spent the past decade of my professional life as a field researcher. Initially, I didn't know how to describe what I was doing. My first ten years beyond high school were spent in the US military, first as a Naval Academy midshipman and then a Marine Corps infantry officer. In the summer of 2004, during a combat tour in Iraq, I decided if I made it back home in one piece, I wanted to get paid to travel and write for the rest of my life. I thought the only people who fit that job description were called foreign correspondents, and I spent the first three years of my postmilitary career striving to become one.

My assumption was wrong. Many professionals get paid to travel and write, and few of them, particularly in the twenty-first century, seem to be journalists. Thanks to Facebook, Twitter, and Google Translate, the market for foreign correspondents has never been lower. International bureau chiefs are still around, but news services rely more on local aggregated content from worldwide social media than on hired staff to identify and distribute major events in real time. The few foreign correspondents left are working twice as hard to find stories and get field time. With the internet driving international news cycles, the luster and mystique associated with the title, even for the largest media organizations, will never be what it once was.

Despite those limitations, I spent two years as a freelance writer, dispatching stories from both foreign and domestic locales. In 2007, I traversed the entire length of the US-Mexico border for the better part of three months, a journey that framed the substance of my second book. As interviews and observations yielded new and unexpected discoveries, I sensed that my field research on the US-Mexico border enabled me to better understand borders in general. I didn't know what it meant, but it suggested I might have a future in research beyond journalistic curiosity.

When *The Border* was published in the fall of 2008, drug violence seemed to be gripping northern Mexico and financial calamity had stricken global markets. The book didn't sell many copies, but—to my surprise—I had suddenly been branded as a border expert. A colleague at the US State Department asked me to join a small team of specialists from different fields who assessed security and international border conditions worldwide through interviews and field observation, delivering their written reports within two weeks of returning.

In keeping with my original ambitions, I spent the next two years being paid to travel and write. But unlike in journalism, my data collection and published work were exclusively for private clients. At that time, many were affiliated with the United States government, but a handful of academic and corporate organizations were also interested in my research. Most reports I wrote were labeled "for official use only," as were the interviews or debriefing sessions I participated in following international travel. As I meandered around the world, I met hundreds of other people who were traveling and writing their own nonpublic reports, most often for universities, governments, nonprofits, or multinational corporations. I learned that many more field researchers get paid to travel and write than foreign correspondents.

By formal nondisclosure agreement and informal decorum, I was obligated as an independent contractor to avoid publicly discussing most of my work. Even so, I was professionally thriving. In addition to field research projects, my earlier US-Mexico border work started drawing interest from several academic and government institutions. In 2009, I joined the Foreign Policy Research Institute as a senior fellow, with a research focus on northern Mexico. In 2011, I was appointed as the policy and planning director for US Customs and Border Protection. Both opportunities unfolded because of my field research experience.

In the Marine Corps, I was told no professional skill was mastered unless it had been learned, done, and taught. When I returned to the private sector in 2012, I proposed a field research program to my think tank colleagues. The program's purpose was not to discuss theories about field research origins or debate the merits of qualitative versus quantitative methodology. The goal was simple: to make better international field researchers.

Collaborating with experts who ranged from corporate ethnographers to professional anthropologists, I spent the next two years designing and testing a curriculum that could be scaled from individuals to large research teams. A third of the material derived from Marine Corps concepts that I found instrumental to field research success. Another third drew from practical lessons learned during the decade I had been traveling to collect data—street smarts often classified as "common sense" that, all too often, are uncommon. The final third was built from guidebooks, literature reviews, and best-practice discussions with other professionals.

Discoveries in the field invariably happen in both deliberate and unforeseen places. Field research involves structured data collection and analysis but also includes experiences ranging from tapas parties to taxicab conversations. Education can unfold in classrooms, conferences, and cafés—all in equally robust forms. Answers to our research questions—the stuff we are looking to find—are shaped through realities we didn't know existed before we encountered new things. As we travel to learn, traveling itself becomes learning.

Experienced international researchers often tell novices that the only way to learn how to learn the processes of observing, interviewing, compiling, summarizing, and presenting field research is to "get out in the field." But what exactly are they supposed to be doing once they are there? How do professional researchers learn these skills effectively while also maximizing the likelihood that they could complete their research without hazarding their health? What inherent cultural limitations do researchers have, and how do they handle them?

When we travel to learn, we seek an experience that will alter our perceptions and teach us something we didn't know. Clients, employers, or educational institutions pay us well to find information and bring back insights. When we purchase the ticket and board the plane—whether it is to study abroad, complete a dissertation, finish a corporate report, analyze a policy option, or write an article—we intuitively know we are going to come back from the trip a different person.

This handbook covers the before, during, and after of field research. The first part reviews concepts, ideas, and skills that are important to internalize before embarking on a professional project. The second section considers practical, realistic scenarios for the day-to-day tactics of working in the field. The final chapters advise researchers on preparing and delivering their material and coping with reentry after returning home.

If you're looking for a deconstruction of theories about qualitative or quantitative research, you've come to the wrong place and the wrong person. I'm a practitioner, not an academic. What motivates me, and inspired this book, is a passion for learning how to learn, especially in the field.

This handbook is humbly offered to prepare you for that experience.

Note

1.   David M. Newman, *Studyguide for Sociology: Exploring the Architecture of Everyday Life*, Just the Facts 101, accessed January 28, 2016, www.jtf101.com.

PART I
Research Preparation

1

Framing the "Other"

You've hatched the plan, been given a budget, and accepted the assignment. Your project is taking you across the border, perhaps overseas. Maybe it is your first time out of the country; perhaps you have toured the world on student visits or family vacations. One way or another, the mysterious joys and demands of the twenty-first-century world's flatness and permanent connectivity are taking you somewhere abroad. You're going into the field.

And you are by no means alone. In 2012, according to the United Nations World Tourism Organization, people crossed international borders over one billion times. That number has quadrupled since 1970, when the organization logged 250 million trips from one country to another, and increased forty times since 1960, from 25 million.[1] Combined with the internet's ability to collect and distribute information about another country, an extraordinary number of people are seeing, experiencing, and researching foreign places.

Why Do Field Research?

The normalcy of this exposure to travel provides the field researcher with an unconventional professional challenge. The amount of information anyone can easily access on other countries through the internet is staggering and can make any research director or program manager question the value of sending someone into the field in the first place. Internet queries can tell us the demographic breakdown of Burkina Faso and the price of mulberries in Bhutan. What could possibly be so important about going to either place just to investigate these topics?

While experienced field researchers believe the answer to that question is self-evident, suspicion often lingers in the minds of supervisors that "research" is actually a ruse for vacation, adventure, or search for spiritual meaning in less materialistic locales. While any or all of these experiences may be a byproduct of research, they are not the real reasons you are going.

So why are you going? Whether for professional or personal reasons, you believe—rightfully—that no amount of time in the library or on the laptop studying a place can substitute for being there. Reading about Burkina Faso's demographics cannot enable you to understand the way tribe, climate, terrain, language, soil, clan, colonialism, and family variables shape those demographics. Looking up the price of Bhutan's mulberries won't teach you why they are grown, what factors drive price fluctuations, who buys them and why, if they are purchased openly or on the black market, or what makes them valuable as exports to neighboring nations.

"Showing up is 80 percent of life," said Woody Allen. Fieldwork is no different. Properly done, field research is about much more than finding answers; it leads to discovering the questions you never knew to ask.

An Art and a Science

Most academic field research manuals describe existing fieldwork literature in methodological terms and focus on procedural, ethical, and scientific aspects. These typically include, but are not limited to, lessons on how to make surveys, legal and moral considerations, techniques for collecting information, scaling sample sizes, assessing and sorting data, and presenting conclusions. That is all important stuff, and we should unquestionably study and attend to it as we learn the skills of our trade.

Field research, however, is more than science. As Harry F. Wolcott's *The Art of Fieldwork* says, there's more to the process than developing a clear hypothesis and testing it through a scientific method. "Science is perhaps best recognized as a critical aspect of the art of fieldwork," writes Wolcott. "That is a different view than one that holds science to be kingpin in the fieldwork endeavor."[2] If Wolcott is right, aspiring field researchers must learn more than scientific methodology; they must see themselves in an apprenticeship as an artist.

This is a challenge because the art of field research requires skills and experience not conventionally taught in the academic world. "We cannot teach students to be artists," writes Dr. Jakub Grygiel, describing the relevance of fieldwork to policy. "We can only teach them to appreciate art."[3] We can learn to replicate scientific, quantifiable processes. Literature reviews, data collection, map studies, and online research can all be done through classroom expertise. But fieldwork demands something more: an exploratory inquisitiveness to investigate what will lead to the right data, empathy to persuade interviewees to trust researchers with (often sensitive) information, and sufficient aptitude to work professionally and return home safely. As with the writer, the painter, the sculptor, and the poet, so also does the field researcher learn through time and experience to recognize and understand the skills and methods governing the craft.

Taking a Walk and Beginning Reconnaissance

Dr. George Friedman, founder of Stratfor, a geopolitical risk and forecasting company, illustrates the limitations he sees with learning about a place just by studying geography on a map and explains how they are overcome when discovering a place in person. "Walking a mountain path in the Carpathians in November, where bandits move about today as they did centuries ago, teaches me why this region will never be completely tamed or easily captured," Friedman writes. "A drive through the Polish countryside near Warsaw will remind me why Napoleon, Hitler and Stalin took the path they did, and why Poland thinks the way it does."[4]

In this way, field research can often be seen as the first phase, rather than the last, in problem solving. Marine Corps instructors teach junior officers that basic leadership requires a cycle of planning, arranging for and doing reconnaissance, finishing a plan, tasking, and supervising. Of the six "troop leading steps," two involve organizing and completing reconnaissance, which is much less mysterious than it sounds. Finding information is what field research is all about. And if that sounds like spy work, well . . . the skill sets required for both field research and intelligence collection have far more similarities than differences.

Shedding Bias

Considering their resemblances, both field researchers and intelligence collectors of any background—government, corporate, or academic—will benefit from grounding their professional endeavors in an understanding of bias and perception. How will the people you are researching perceive you when you're in the field? How will you perceive them? What natural biases will impact your ability to ask and answer honest questions? How does your background enhance or reduce your capacity to collect the data your project requires?

Shedding bias isn't fully possible. We are all inclined, through culture and experience, to view the world in a certain way. But stepping back, examining, and evaluating the way their own race, ethnicity, citizenship, culture, nationality, gender, sexual orientation, physical appearance, body language, speech patterns, and value sets will be seen by the people they want to meet with in the field enables researchers of any background to acquire new perspectives on their abilities and themselves. Our biases can evolve, but they will always exist.

Although this may seem intuitive, academic conversations about charged subjects like racial bias, ethnic preference, and gender discrimination often lead to heated debates on social privilege, class warfare, and policy failures. Hashing out these disputes is not the field researcher's motivation; polemics and political correctness have no place in good fieldwork. But without understanding your natural bias, it's difficult to look for the data you might be missing.

Bias can emerge as part of a project itself, as sociologist Sudhir Venkatesh learned during his first days as a graduate student. While researching his first project, Venkatesh was surprised to discover that many of the researchers who were most intent on collecting statistical data on the poor had no real interest in meeting the people they wrote about. "On one side of the divide lay a beautifully manicured Gothic campus, with privileged students, most of them white, walking to class and playing sports," he writes in *Gang Leader for a Day*. "On the other side were down-and-out African Americans offering cheap labor and services (changing oil, washing windows, selling drugs) or panhandling on street corners."[5]

You don't need to go into the field to find what you already know, or even necessarily what you know you don't know. That part can happen through literature reviews, online research, and phone or Skype interviews with the right people. Field research, in contrast, tells you what you *don't know you don't know*. This is why it is important to examine your own expectations. As a field researcher, understanding the bias your own life experience has created gives you a head start on identifying the unknowns—things you don't know you don't know—before leaving the comforts of the library, classroom, or office.

Who Are the Nacirema?

Have you ever heard of the Nacirema? Anthropology and sociology students often study the tribe's body ritual as an early course requirement. Each morning, Nacirema tribe members enter a shrine room, bow their head before a charm box, and mingle holy water that has been purified from the local Water Temple to perform a rite of ablution. A ritual is also performed daily involving a small bundle inserted into the mouth and then moving the bundle—along with a magical powder-based substance—in a formalized series of gestures. The Nacirema sometimes embark on fasting to make fat people thin or ceremonial feasting to make thin people fat. Excretion and reproduction are formalized, routinized, and relegated to secrecy.[6]

Spelled backward, you may have noticed, Nacirema is *American*. Perhaps you never considered washing your face or brushing your teeth as "body rituals," but how do you think they would appear to someone who had never seen them before? What about other common American physical practices, such as regular visits to the doctor and dentist or taking sick people to the hospital?

The point of the exercise is not to judge these activities as good or bad. Face washing and teeth brushing are not the only practices humans have performed throughout history prior to sleep or when waking up. The value of studying the Nacirema lies with admitting that the way modern Americans do things—even common daily physical activities—is an adopted cultural practice. If we aspire to make the unfamiliar familiar to our colleagues, students, readers, or supervisors—which is the goal of field research in the first place—we must first start by making the familiar unfamiliar to ourselves.

Who Is the Other?

Making the familiar unfamiliar—as with the Nacirema illustration—leads us to an awareness and understanding of the "Other." Philosophy and social science characterize the Other as the social construction of an ethnicity, culture, or nationality that is different from your own, "a state of being different than the identity of self or social identities."[7] Seeing a "them" as opposite to an "us" has played an important conceptual role in how scholars from Edward Said to Simone de Beauvoir explain human relationships. More works from social science theory than can be listed discuss how "Othering" creates ethnocentrism, or the belief that one's own ethnic group (or nation, culture, gender, etc.) is superior to others' as well as defining meaning to the "Others" using your own self or social identity as a standard.

Why is this important? Understanding the Other matters to the field researcher because if you're going into the field, some form of the Other is most likely your research topic. At some level, the root of any research project must begin with awareness that the unknown is not better or worse but simply contextual. Reconsidering daily hygiene as a tribal ritual is not the only method for field researchers to reflect on their own cultural experiences. It is instead a useful starting point to begin the process of reevaluating the Other before leaving the country.

The point is not to debate the merits or flaws of your own culture versus another but to define how to succeed as a field researcher. Your academic, professional, and personal experiences are part of what you bring to the field. And conversely, from the perspective of the people you're researching, the Other is you.

From a glittering university campus in Zurich to a dynamic, vibrant slum in Mumbai, from an expatriate nightclub in Nairobi to a border checkpoint in Iraqi Kurdistan, successful qualitative field research includes mixing the systematic collection of tangible information with the intangible process of navigating interpersonal relationships. No matter where you go in the world, someone sees you as an "Other," even as you are encountering them in the same way. As you discover yourself, identify your own bias, and understand how you create "the Other," the research questions you started with will change.

Clear Eyes, Full Hearts

No academic credential is necessary to learn how to look at the world. "One sees clearly only with the heart," Antoine de Saint-Exupéry's *Little Prince* tells us. "Anything essential is invisible to the eyes."[8] Willfully shedding one's sense of cultural superiority is the first step to removing the scales.

Each nation is more than a single culture; most contain hundreds, perhaps even thousands, of subcultures. Explore them firsthand, not just through books or the internet. Go into the countryside if you were raised in the city. Walk through an ethnic neighborhood different from your own. Spend a weekend in the desert if you grew up near the ocean. As you absorb and discover, ask yourself about your observations. What do you talk with people about and why? What facts about the new place do you notice? What about this region is common to your own, and what is different? Where are the parallels? Where are the contrasts?

This is where your research starts and how your research questions will evolve. The questions you start with will not be the same ones you will end up answering. The first time I traveled along the US-Mexico border in 2007, the mayor of Eagle Pass, Texas, casually mentioned to me that "everyone knows the Rio Grande starts in Mexico." Every map I

had previously seen, which framed my inherent bias, had told me the Rio
Grande's source was in the United States. But sure enough, as soon as I
traveled north of the confluence of the Rio Grande and Rio Cónchos—a
river that flows through northern Mexico and joins the Rio Grande south
of Presidio, Texas—the Rio Grande was shallow. I had no idea the river's primary source was in another country, and that discovery led to new
questions.

So start simple. Make your initial field research goals big and clear.
Understand how Moldovans see Russia, for example. Learn about gender
relations in Zimbabwe. As with any art, the medium will take you in a different direction than you may expect. The field will change and shape you
by exposing you to things you had no idea you didn't know.

George Friedman describes how he walks around a city where he does
not speak the language. As you read his description below, ask, Does this
look like a passive stroll? Does it sound as if he has shed an ethnocen-
tric—or self-centric—perspective? Does this sound like a tourist or a
field researcher?

Go to the places where the people you will never hear of live. Find
a school and see the children leave at the end of the day. You want
the schools where there is pushing and shoving and where an older
brother comes to walk their sister home. You are now where you
should be. Look at their shoes. Are they old or new? Are they local
or from the global market? Are they careful with them as if they
were precious or casual with them as they kick a ball around? Watch
children play after school and you can feel the mood and tempo of
a neighborhood.

Go past the apartments people live in. Smell them. The un-
healthy odor of decay or sewage tells you about what they must endure in their lives. Are there banks in the neighborhood? If not,
there isn't enough business there to build one. The people are living paycheck to paycheck. In the cafes where men meet, are they
older men, retired? Or are they young men? Are the cafes crowded
with men in their forties drinking tea or coffee, going nowhere? Are
they laughing and talking or sitting quietly as if they have nothing
left to say?

Official figures on unemployment can be off a number of ways.
But when large numbers of 40-year-old men have nothing to
do, then the black economy—the one that pays no taxes and isn't

counted by the government but is always there and important—isn't pulling the train. Are the police working in pairs or alone? What kind of weapons do they carry? Are they everywhere, nowhere or have just the right presence?
There are endless things you can learn if you watch.[9]

Key Points

- Information technology makes it easy for researchers to believe they are asking adequate questions when they have used only online research or video interviews as sources. Field research does not replace these methods; it supports and enhances them.
- Field research is both an art and a science. Methods of science can be taught, but an art has to be learned through practice and appreciation.
- Field research is not just about testing hypotheses, collecting data, or finding answers. It is about researchers learning what they did not know they needed to know.
- If done properly, field research often results in questions that the researcher would never have known were important to ask.
- Field research enables leaders to make better decisions because they have a more accurate and thorough understanding of on-the-ground information.
- Field research works best if applied toward the beginning of a problem-solving process rather than at the end.
- The first step in fieldwork preparation is evaluating the way your own race, ethnicity, citizenship, culture, nationality, gender, sexual orientation, physical appearance, body language, speech patterns, and value sets will be perceived by the people you want to meet with in the field.
- The second step in fieldwork preparation is to understand your natural and inherent bias as objectively as possible relative to the variables listed above.
- The "Other," which originated as a philosophical term, refers to the social construction of a specific ethnicity, culture, or nationality that is different from, outside of, or exclusive from your own.
- Field researchers must caution against "Othering," which leads to ethnocentrism, or believing that one's own bias is superior to "the Other," while in the field.

- Start with simple research questions and make initial field research goals as broad as possible. Simplicity helps a field researcher learn to identify and shed bias.

Notes

1. Elizabeth Becker, *Overbooked: The Exploding Business of Travel and Tourism* (New York: Simon & Schuster, 2013), 17.

2. Harry Wolcott, *The Art of Fieldwork* (Lanham, MD: AltaMira, 2005), 12.

3. Jakub Grygiel, "Educating for National Security," *Orbis* (Spring 2013): 211.

4. George Friedman, "A Geopolitical Journey: The Traveler," Stratfor, November 8, 2010.

5. Sudhir Venkatesh, *Gang Leader for a Day: A Rogue Sociologist Takes to the Streets* (New York: Penguin, 2008), 2.

6. H. M. Miner, "Body Ritual among the Nacirema," *American Anthropologist* 58 (June 1956): 503–507.

7. J. Miller, "Otherness," in *The SAGE Encyclopedia of Qualitative Research* (Thousand Oaks, CA: SAGE Publications, 2008), 587–88.

8. Antoine de Saint-Exupéry, *The Little Prince* (New York: Harcourt, 1971), 63.

9. Friedman, "A Geopolitical Journey."

2

Developing Your
Research Style

On August 17, 2015, *Washington Post* staff writer Christopher Ingraham published a short blog post on the newspaper's website: "Every County in America Ranked by Scenery and Climate." Using an aggregate data map from the United States Department of Agriculture's Natural Amenities Scale, which rates and ranks US counties on scenery and climate, Ingraham declared Red Lake County, Minnesota, as the "absolute worst place to live in America."[1]

In the United States, the article generated outrage among Minnesotans, and not simply because Ingraham insulted their home state. If his byline had been filed from Minneapolis, or even from Chicago, residents might not have argued. But his dispatch was posted from Washington, DC, using a data map assessing places that he never saw in person. Ingraham had committed the worst sin any researcher can make: issuing a declarative, qualitative statement about a place without ever having been there.

Ingraham's thought patterns—from data collection to presented hypothesis—are more typical of twenty-first-century research efforts than many might like to admit. Claiming a particular region is "the worst place to live" seems inappropriate behavior for a researcher (or journalist, consultant, student, or any professional fact-finder) without having collected any data from said location. Field research inherently requires traveling into the field (for our purposes, this means outside your home country), and, as we have learned, our identity influences the choices we make when planning our project.

Positionality and Professional Bias

In the previous chapter, we learned about recognizing, considering, and identifying our biases. Another way of describing this is *positionality*, the idea that important aspects of our identity—gender, race, ethnicity, and class—define our relational positions and normative assumptions as we record observations, collect data, and conduct interviews.[2] It is easy to understand the relevance of identifying positionality when accomplishing fieldwork. Our challenge is going one step further: learning how to use positionality to our advantage.

Our personalities, genders, ethnicities, cultures, and experiences—in addition to the specifics of our professional research obligations—can and will enable each researcher to cultivate his or her own individual research style. Field research isn't a one-size-fits-all process, and choosing the right approach to a project is a technique you can choose to cultivate by developing your own style. By reflecting on your bias and understanding its relationship to your research abilities, you can and will enable yourself to prepare for the field every day.

As we have seen, reflecting on our position relative to others enables us to understand why we see the world the way we do and to consider how our observations might differ from others. Predispositions are inevitable—they are neither good nor bad. Our tendencies and preferences will inevitably affect every aspect of our research styles. Our goal is to learn, understand, and develop them.

Beyond positionality, another inescapable reality for anyone completing a field research project is one's professional background and training. Academic, government, and corporate researchers (a typology we will use throughout this book) each have both formal and informal requirements, processes, and cultural norms for traveling internationally to collect qualitative data. Each structure within these general research arenas shapes the experiences a researcher is likely to have and generates both opportunities and limitations when researchers are in the field for any length of time.

To understand and utilize the benefits of our identities and research obligations, let's consider different reasons you might have for going into the field. Are you completing an anthropology dissertation? Examining the quality of this year's cacao crop? Collecting data on cybercrime response capabilities? Leading an undergraduate study abroad group? Querying agricultural leaders on tractor usage? Analyzing an international border's security structure? Interviewing human smugglers? Investigating a competing brand? Identifying community, ethnic, and tribal leaders in relationship to your political goals?

The examples of possible field assignments above denote research I have either done myself or known someone to have done. The list is representative, not exhaustive; your field research project might involve any one of these things, or—more likely—something similar but also different. Some research jobs might involve all of these broad categories; some will involve two; almost all will include at least one.

Comparing and contrasting academic, government, and corporate field research objectives helps a prospective researcher identify the preconceptions inherent to specific institutions. Each of these types of organizations generally wants something different, and tailoring your style with an awareness of how demands from fieldwork can vary enables the best possible end product.

Academic Research: The Limitations of Overqualification

Most methodologies, practices, and customs in modern academic field research have relatively recent origins in social sciences. As anthropology and sociology grew in stature as academic disciplines in the late nineteenth and early twentieth centuries, Margaret Mead's *Coming of Age in Samoa* (1928) was among the first works to exemplify what social scientists later began calling "participant observation."[3] Mead spent much of 1925 interviewing young Samoan women about sexual practices and documenting her observations of tribal social structures. She highlighted how Western practices differed from her own observations in Samoa, noting in detail how her conclusions were interpretive and based, in part, on her own cultural experiences.

Academic field research, especially in anthropology, tends to be romanticized. Anthropological fieldwork is usually described as ethnography, the study of people that "is to the cultural or social anthropologist what lab research is to the biologist."[4] Ethnographic fieldwork is framed to students as a formalized and specialized process that can be accomplished only after completing extensive academic training. "Most anthropologists begin their preparation with several years of study in the history and previous ethnographic literature of the region in which they propose to do fieldwork," write John Monaghan and Peter Just in *Social and Cultural Anthropology*. "An ethnographer may need to acquire at least passable fluency in several languages. In addition to such general preparation, ethnographers are usually trained in more specialized fields concerning the kind of problem they intend to investigate."[5]

In some academic circles, fieldwork completed prior to earning a doctorate (which would suggest one is "fully qualified") is looked down on as borderline unprofessional. The graduate student researcher, in the academic view, may have rushed into the field without being properly trained. An undergraduate researcher might almost be seen as a professional anthropologist's nightmare: someone entirely unqualified to handle the specific methodological requirements yet having the audacity to consider themselves worthy of fieldwork.

Indeed, many undergraduates are not well qualified to do field research—but many academics with doctorates are not very good either. The benefits of social science education, literature reviews, language training, and specialized coursework cannot be discounted in preparation. But ultimately, despite the focus on methodology and process, the most successful academic field researchers I have met echo the same refrain: the only way to succeed at fieldwork is to stop studying about the field and just get started. It is a cliché because it's true: one cannot swim without getting wet.

For example, Margaret Mead's field research contributed to some of the ideas that led to our understanding of bias and "Othering" we explored in the previous chapter. At the same time, her ability to do field research wasn't necessarily enabled by her academic qualifications. Mead had a keen eye, a creative spirit, and a curious mind. Her conclusions about alternative sexual practices, and the resulting challenges posed to Western sexual mores, were exceptionally controversial in the late 1920s and, in subsequent decades, fueled several critiques of her methodology. Derek Freeman, an anthropologist who had also done fieldwork in Samoa, derided Mead as a naive dilettante, critiquing not only her conclusions but the interviewing style she used to reach them. "It's hard to see how Mead's work in Samoa can be now viewed as anything but a pretty fable," concluded Rob Lightner, who reviewed Freeman's *The Fateful Hoaxing of Margaret Mead* in 1999 for Amazon.[6]

The Mead-Freeman dispute roiled academic and anthropological circles enough that it eventually garnered its own work, *The Trashing of Margaret Mead: Anatomy of an Anthropological Controversy*. In his book, anthropologist Paul Shankman deconstructs the controversy, coming down on Mead's side as a "decent, careful fieldworker," and concludes that Freeman was, "frankly, a nutcake."[7] Both Mead and Freeman had been trained as fieldworkers, both had worked in Samoa, and both had probably made mistakes. But Shankman favors Mead because of what he described as her own modesty toward her fieldwork and respectful demeanor to her academic opponents. In 1976, at the annual American Anthropological Association meeting, Mead denounced a resolution to condemn competing critiques of her work, calling such actions "book burning." Freeman, conversely, was known to contact universities and demand they revoke the PhDs of his opponents.[8]

Succeeding as a field researcher is about more than theories. Emphasizing methodological rigor can result in an arrogance rooted in the perception of expertise that is really just a thin veneer covering the fear of stumbling through a PhD defense or facing a peer review. Mead's field research has endured beyond the invective of her critics (and she had many) not merely because of how she was trained but even more because of her own awareness of her positionality and the context that created with her respondents and environment. This knowledge enabled her to document her observations, collect her data, and examine the evidence without agenda, which strengthened her challenge to conventions. Doing this required action, not training.

Margaret Mead understood her own biases—not only as an individual but from her own academic training—explained them in her work, and pushed to cross beyond the boundaries they had imposed during her field research. Although these are essential components to academic field-work, no course can ever fully teach them nor can an institution confer them with a degree. Mead's academic abilities were noteworthy, but her enduring accomplishments owe as much, or more, to her awareness of her positionality as to her professional qualifications.

Corporate Research: Going beyond the Bottom Line

In academic field research, the overemphasis on training can generate limitations from an obsession with methods, theories, and qualifications over basic skills, respectful courtesies, and common sense. Corporate field research, on the other hand, has a high demand for finding data that delivers immediate results. Markets change quickly, and complex algorithms, pricing models, and computing systems can move financial profiles, quarterly projections, and bottom lines in seconds. The most relevant variable for defining success in the field is not professional training but market impact.

Corporations—both publicly traded and privately owned—that invest in field research do so because they need specific information that cannot be discovered from headquarters. Whatever the information is, it is usually proprietary. Because of this, corporate field research—even when contracted through consulting firms or freelancers—depends heavily on personal trust and relationship management.[9]

As noted, corporate field research also depends on timeliness. One consumer foods field researcher I know was required to persuade a menial fast food employee of a competitor to reveal recipes of specific ingredients. The information had to be obtained unexpectedly and quickly in preparation for a meeting with a product distributor the next day. The data revealed a difference between the product the researcher's competitor sold to fast food retailers and one sold in stores through the distributor. The distributor switched to the researcher's company because of the revelation.

The consumer foods sleuth was a part-time researcher who was employed by the company full-time under another job description—a common occurrence in corporate field research. In a corporate context, executives usually reserve field research assignments for trusted employees. How fast the information is obtained may matter less than confidence in the accuracy and source of the product. Corporate field research, also called corporate intelligence, is perhaps more like what many of us consider spy work than most formal government research.

While on a project in Turkmenistan, I chatted for two hours with a salesman from an agricultural equipment company. His business card said he was a "Product and Marketing Specialist" with the "Worldwide Agricultural Equipment Division." He had traveled to over one hundred countries, and his work was less about sales than about researching industry trends and forecasting opportunities. What got him the initial field research job, he told me, was the reputation he had as a loyal, trustworthy, and discreet employee. He liked agricultural field research, and most people in the company didn't want to travel internationally. In six years, he had become one of only three employees for his multinational company who was doing fieldwork. His reports carried as much leverage at corporate headquarters as a diplomatic ambassador's dispatches to a minister of foreign affairs.

Freelance field researchers can often work in a long-term capacity with clients whose services involve specific commodities. The levels of technical knowledge for corporate specialists are often difficult to learn, and field researchers can find themselves serving as industry middlemen. In Bamako, Mali, I met a multilingual gold expert who had dual citizenship in Portugal and Angola. For almost a year he had been connecting gold miners in Mali's mountains with international buyers. A friend had taught him the business, and both miners and exporters trusted him. Although he was in good shape, hiking into the mountains was exhausting.

Later that season, he planned to return to Europe and become an industry adviser, then come back in the field every few months to maintain his expertise.

The agricultural specialist and gold middleman both demonstrated an ability to influence the bottom line by developing depth in specialized knowledge. When corporate employees travel internationally for business meetings, they often follow a planned itinerary with very specific requirements on what they will see, eat, and do. Consulting local tourism websites, the executive's smartphone is locked to his or her face, moving from one objective on the itinerary to another, with barely room to breathe.

Skilled corporate field research, in contrast, is about knowing specific information at an opportune moment. Depending on the situation, corporate field research may be necessary for acquiring rapid facts, or it could be more about substantive data collected over time. Taking advantage of every data-collection opportunity available produces the timely, accurate results corporate research requires to gain competitive advantage in meetings and markets.

Government Research: Seeing Past the Politics

Every government in the world, as well as most nongovernmental organizations that influence policy and politics, conducts field research. It is called fact finding, intelligence collection, or (if it involves investment in another country or multinational institution) program evaluation. The tools can include assessments, investigations, and information requirements. The deliverables all involve directly contacting people and going to places. This is the final category of field research, and one that needs careful consideration. Given our inherent cultural biases, and the function of government in representing power, work done for governments often promulgates—awkward verb intended—the biggest bias of all.

Any professional, ethnic, religious, or cultural organization with a public policy agenda—including, but not limited to, governments—has predispositions we must understand. First and foremost, almost every information-collection activity that could impact public policy operates from the angle of seeking facts that reinforce the organization's policy agenda or government's point of view.[10] This includes every "nonpartisan" think tank and government-funded research institution, no matter how independent it claims to be. Whether you are an American, German, Russian, Chinese, or Samoan government fact-finder, it would be unprofessional not to know what the institution, organization, or person paying you already thinks, feels, and believes. It is equally unprofessional not to acknowledge this has some impact on your research plan.

As an example, consider the field research completed from 2002 to 2004 to evaluate and search for the Iraqi dictator Saddam Hussein's alleged weapons of mass destruction programs prior to and after the US military invasion. In 2002, with each new United Nations inspection mission sent to Iraq, public pronouncements from US political and military officials made it clear that the accuracy of information about potential weapons of mass destruction mattered less than how each new discovery impacted political choices and public perceptions. By 2004, after the regime had been dispatched, investigations went from looking for nuclear or chemical weapons to figuring out why they weren't there. Each fact-finding mission, capability investigation, or program assessment had an obvious policy agenda. Any claim otherwise was, and remains, patently false.

Political influencers may assert they are merely looking for facts on the ground, but field research can often be merely a tool to fit a previously scripted agenda. Governments have policies to promulgate, and non-profit policy organizations have donors (or government research program managers) to whom they must report. Official government researchers experience different power dynamics than academic fieldworkers with interviewees, who might be more likely to woo the researcher's favor in the hopes of receiving favorable policy treatment.[11] For the government field researcher, there may be practical and ethical ramifications for disclosing these interests in interviews—including academic researchers on government sponsorship—but that is a topic for a later chapter. For our purposes now, we must acknowledge the inherent limitations policy agendas place on government field researchers.

Considering Your Style

Examining the origins of professional bias is not to suggest the academic researcher should be less careful about methods, or the corporate researcher less aware of market forces, or the government official less conscious of preferred policies. Remember, positionality is neither good nor bad: it is a set of variables every field researcher must understand, analyze, and use to his or her advantage. Additionally, knowing the norms across research fields helps a field researcher cultivate a style to fit the right situation.

Developing a research style isn't difficult. Anyone doing fieldwork can and will do so. It is, however, a deliberate process. Finding your research style cannot happen until you actually start researching—often with an eye toward (if not an assignment from) one of the three industries we have examined.

As you start this process with an open mind, you will instinctively learn to balance your industry's bias. You will notice academic researchers can risk emphasizing methods while excluding the political and economic skills mere amateurs can bring to the process. Corporate researchers might instinctively discard anything that doesn't impact their profit and loss statements and miss an opportunity to learn relevant cultural data. Government researchers may be so intent on pushing a policy agenda that they fail to observe (or prevent their fieldworkers from publishing) facts that might make them change course.

There's more to overcoming inherent bias than striving for cultural literacy or understanding the professional background to your research assignment. Thanks to the internet, learning facts and figures about your travel destination is the easy part. The process of acknowledging positionality, both personal and professional, leads a researcher to understand the distinctive signature he or she brings into the field. We will talk about using your style throughout the rest of the book; for now, just remember that your personal research style is what we want to convert our bias (or positionality) into through study and practice.

Let me illustrate, comparing how my own personal style matches up with one of the greats. For many reasons, I could never be Margaret Mead. Beyond my lack of anthropological training and my military background, I'm also a bald, brawny, white, heterosexual American man. I cannot imagine any scenario in which young Samoan women—or, let's be honest, their fathers, brothers, or uncles—would let me interview them about their sexuality. Even if I were linguistically, culturally, and scholastically trained for a decade, the thought that I could ever conduct research the way Mead did on female sexuality is improbable at best.

But those same qualities that would prevent some research opportunities can enable others. My background enables me to collect all kinds of data from former military personnel, law enforcement agents, government bureaucrats, policy wonks, wannabe rogues, and regular dudes around the world with a relaxed ease that I feel confident Margaret Mead could never match in certain environments. This is not because I am a better-trained researcher. Rather, it is because I have developed my research style by acknowledging my positionality and building on what I know. We can use situations where we naturally feel comfortable to our advantage and let others teach us as we collect their insights.

Developing Your Style

How can you start developing a research style? First, be patient. Slowing down in anything—eating, walking, speaking, learning, and, yes, traveling—takes conscious effort. For the traveler, one way of sustaining the illusion of control when entering new environments is staying busy. Speed is one way new travelers sometimes respond to stress, and this makes activity seem important for day-to-day survival. But blazing through a travel itinerary inhibits the type of learning that enhances your work. Yes, your meetings are essential. But scheduling one or two engagements instead of five or six will make your time more, not less, productive.

Second, start small. Start where you live. Find a street, neighborhood, or town within walking, biking, or driving distance. Go there. Walk around and notice how people react to you. Eat lunch and talk to the people who are serving you. Sit in a bar and strike up conversation. Notice what people are wearing and why.

Now put yourself in their shoes. What was it like to grow up here? What would it feel like to move here—wherever here is—from another region or country? How would you get around if you didn't speak the language? What customs would you have to learn if you weren't part of the dominant ethnic group? What cultural norms would you have to adopt to get work, be accepted in the community, and feel safe in your daily life?

Now write it down. Use an ink pen and scribble in a notebook. Handwriting your field notes engages different parts of your brain, and the physical interaction of pen and paper in a private place preserves your experience and observations for later reflection. Audio and video recordings work too, but the practice of taking field notes is a basic research skill. Novice researchers write down far less of their daily observation than they realize, and failing to practice the discipline of noting thoughts is an amateur's hallmark. Take notes. And read them.[12]

Next, do the same thing on a different scale. If you were raised in an urban area, go somewhere rural; if in the country, go to a city. But when you go, do not just tour a cattle ranch or snap a selfie at a skyscraper. Spend a day or two doing the same thing described above. Note how people dress and talk to each other. Compare and contrast with behaviors you have previously observed. Write about how a new place makes you feel compared to a familiar one. Note similarities and differences.

Consider this advice from Michael Perry, a rural writer who provides an outstanding description of his suggestions for first-time visitors to towns like his:

> Approach any small town with a reverence for what you can learn. Memorize the population sign. Small-town people love to out-small each other, and you must be prepared.
>
> Go to the café, order quietly, and eavesdrop shamelessly. Wander the local cemetery. Study the headstones. Notice which names recur. Note the spans of birth and death. These stratifications of time compose the foundation of the town.
>
> Browse the community bulletin boards and all announcements taped to the gas station door. In short order you will have clues to who has what, who wants what, who can fix your deck, who can stuff your deer, and who can save your soul.
>
> Drive the outskirts. Consider the look of the town in the rearview mirror as opposed to through the windshield, and think about how you feel. More to the point, if you find yourself trapped behind an old man doing thirty-five in a forty-five, don't figure out a way to pass him, figure out a way to *be* him. [13]

If you don't believe me, or Michael Perry, just ask Christopher Ingraham. After Minnesota's statewide outcry, the *Washington Post* writer traveled to Red Lake County one week after his story was published. After his visit, Ingraham recanted his original opinion. "There's perhaps something amiss in a ranking that places Red Lake County at the absolute bottom of the nation when it comes to scenery and climate," he wrote. "I left feeling like I'd barely scratched the surface of all there is to see and know about the county and the people who call it home."[14] Six months later, Ingraham, his wife, and their twin sons moved to Minnesota, resolving to make a home in a place he had once called the nation's worst.[15]

Once you understand how your personal biases are interwoven with your professional assignment, you can consider how to balance out the bias from other perspectives. Think about how to use academic research training when around government officials. Consider public policy questions when working on a corporate project. Contemplate how changes in economic markets could impact your academic fieldwork.

The tactics associated with encountering, observing, and notetaking are among the most fundamental skills for a researcher to master. Make time to practice these habits in familiar environments, and they will become second nature when you go into new ones. And when they do, you're well on your way to developing your research style and using it skillfully in the field.

Key Points

- Another way of describing bias is *positionality*: the idea that important aspects of our identity—gender, race, ethnicity, and class—define our relational positions and normative assumptions as we record observations, collect data, and conduct interviews.
- Our positionality—personalities, genders, ethnicities, cultures, experiences—in addition to the specifics of our professional research obligations, can and will enable each researcher to cultivate his or her own individual research style.
- Academic, government, and corporate researchers, a typology we will use throughout this book, each have both formal and informal requirements, processes, and cultural norms for traveling internationally to collect qualitative data.
- Most methodologies, practices, and customs in modern academic field research, such as ethnography, have relatively recent origins in social sciences. This can often result in a preference for theory over practicality in academic fieldwork.
- Corporate field research has a bias for finding data that delivers immediate results. The only thing relevant to defining success in the field from a corporate viewpoint is not professional training, but financial impact.
- Every government in the world, as well as most nongovernmental organizations that influence policy and politics, conducts field research. This often results in a bias toward existing policies in government-related fieldwork.
- Bias is neither good nor bad: it is a variable every field researcher must understand, analyze, and use to his or her advantage. Knowing the positionality and predispositions of their clients helps field researchers develop their own style to fit the right situation.

- The process of overcoming bias—personal or professional—leads researchers to understand their own style: the distinctive, inimitable signature they bring into the field.
- Slow down and start small as you begin developing your research style.
- Take handwritten notes on your observations in a field notebook. Using pen and paper engages more parts of your brain. Write things down as soon as you possibly can, or you will forget them. Complement this with audio and video recordings as well.
- Once you understand how your personal bias is interwoven with your professional assignment, you can begin to consider how to balance out the bias from other research perspectives.

Notes

1. Christopher Ingraham, "Every County in America, Ranked by Scenery and Climate," *Washington Post*, August 17, 2015, https://www.washingtonpost.com/news /wonk/wp/2015/08/17/every-county-in-america-ranked-by-natural-beauty/.
2. Carl A. Grant and Thandeka K. Chapman, eds., *History of Multicultural Education* (New York: Routledge, 2008), 2:328–29.
3. Carol Bailey, *A Guide to Qualitative Field Research*, 2nd ed. (Thousand Oaks: SAGE Publications, 2006), 8–11.
4. John Monaghan and Peter Just, *Social & Cultural Anthropology* (New York: Oxford University Press, 2000), 13.
5. Ibid., 21.
6. John Horgan, "Margaret Mead's Bashers Owe Her an Apology," *Scientific American*, October 25, 2010, http://blogs.scientificamerican.com/cross-check/margaret -meads-bashers-owe-her-an-apology/.
7. Ibid.
8. Ibid.
9. Carmen Nobel, "Corporate Field Researchers Share Tricks of the Trade," Harvard Business School Working Knowledge, May 26, 2015, http://hbswk.hbs.edu /item/corporate-field-researchers-share-tricks-of-the-trade.
10. Adam Dolnik, *Conducting Terrorism Field Research: A Guide* (New York: Routledge, 2013), 196–99.
11. Ibid., 197.
12. In addition to field notes, this includes *research memoranda*, which can be anything from a detailed documentation of findings to free writing on a notepad on what a field researcher is seeing.
13. Michael Perry, "Population: 562," in *Population: 485: Meeting Your Neighbors One Siren at a Time* (New York: Harper Perennial, 2007), 9.
14. Christopher Ingraham, "I Called This Place 'America's Worst Place to Live.' Then I Went There," *Washington Post*, September 3, 2015, https://www.washington

post.com/news/wonk/wp/2015/09/03/i-called-this-place-americas-worst
-place-to-live-then-i-went-there/. Minnesota residents, and even public officials, had excoriated the *Washington Post* for Ingraham's in absentia verdict and
strongly encouraged him to visit.

15. Christopher Ingraham, "Why I'm Moving to the Place I Called 'America's
Worst Place to Live,'" *Washington Post*, March 8, 2016, https://www.washington
post.com/news/wonk/wp/2016/03/08/why-im-moving-to-the-place-i-called
-americas-worst-place-to-live/.

3

Improving Situational Awareness

You have reflected on your own personal and professional background and explored beyond familiar places. You have recorded observations and chronicled notes in new environments. You do not yet know what to make of the data you've collected, but field research has started feeling comfortable. You have been noticing perspectives you once ignored and are imagining what research might look like in a different country.

Although you feel confident exploring new regions within familiar surroundings, you are still concerned about your personal safety when going to a completely different place. Even in a new part of your country, aspects of your own nation's language, custom, and culture are available as reference points. What you want is to increase that sixth sense of awareness: your personal radar that offers an assurance that you are able to maintain environmental understanding wherever you go. Books, articles, and veteran fieldworkers often repeat that the most important thing to do in a new place is to "keep your situational awareness." What does the term mean? More importantly, how does situational awareness matter to field research?

Situational awareness is a rational, sustained synthesis of instinct and observation—a fusion of cognitive feedback and intangible "feel."[1] Situationally aware people understand the baseline conditions of their environment and pay attention to circumstances that seem out of the ordinary. They know how things are supposed to be under routine conditions and trust the hunches that tell them something is out of place. The phrase implies that you are one step ahead of potential changes—not only as a researcher but as a person. As a skill, awareness is equally relevant to academic, corporate, and government researchers alike.

Observation and Orientation

Although the phrase is relatively recent and has taken on a glib pop culture context (such as articles on how to have "the situational awareness of Jason Bourne"), the concept has origins in United States military theory and doctrine.[2] In the 1980s, US Air Force colonel John Boyd developed and popularized the Observe-Orient-Decide-Act, or OODA, Loop: a cognitive decision-making process every combat leader confronts. In conflict, the side that moves through the OODA Loop with more accuracy, efficiency, and speed, according to Boyd, will be victorious (the idiom of being "in the loop" or "looped in" to information or events is thought to have originated from this same concept).[3]

Seen through the Boyd framework, situational awareness is about the first two components of the loop: observation and orientation. The first component encompasses much of what field research involves: observing what is happening in your immediate environment by paying attention to your surroundings. Orientation is more complicated. It involves identifying choices and available options for actions you can take in your environment to stay safe if you perceive an abnormal event is about to take place.[4]

The methods and techniques we will consider for developing situational awareness are applicable not only in the field, but anywhere. Most of the topical literature comes from security professionals and martial artists. Worldwide, and in the United States in particular, the dramatic increase in terrorism threats and mass shootings over the past two decades in tourist areas, concert venues, shopping malls, schools, workplaces, and other public spaces has driven interest in personal protective tactics. In the world, or in one's home country, very few places can be considered fully safe from violence.

Situational awareness, however, has benefits well beyond avoiding violence. Observing and orienting are not absolute guarantees of safety in any situation, whether at home or traveling. But regardless of the potential threat, such actions are good research practices. Much of the information about situational awareness, after you think about it, appears to be common sense. But putting skills into routine practice is often easier said than done, which is why habits must be formed well in advance to be effective for research or security.

For example, the tactic of sitting with your back to the wall facing the primary entrance and exit is helpful in any closed space, such as a restaurant, meeting room, or conference area. This seat enables you to note the profile, attitude, and likely intent of everyone entering or leaving the space as well as identify possible alternative exits. But simply people watching (observation) doesn't tell you what available options you might have (orientation) if someone you find threatening enters the room. Depending on the situation, options may vary from running toward a possible back entrance, diverting the threat's attention, fighting back, hiding under a table, or sitting calmly and feigning ignorance. Orientation involves considering what your options are and then training those responses to the extent possible in daily life.

Situational awareness doesn't immediately translate into safety without increased, trained reactions of threat response. Studying tactics, which we will describe as behavior domains, will make you more aware, and increased awareness makes your instinctive responses more effective if you feel threatened. Training in the techniques will keep you calm and reactive in an actual threat, which is more likely to lead to better intuitive decision making and more effective actions whenever something out of the ordinary unfolds.

Six Behavior Domains

In *Left of Bang: How the Marine Corps' Combat Hunter Program Can Save Your Life*, Patrick Van Horne and Jason Riley explain how the Marine Corps applied Boyd's theories to develop body language and situational awareness skills in a training program for combat patrolling in Iraq and Afghanistan. The program's goal was simple: keep Marines and civilians alive by identifying and preventing attacks before they happened.[5] Because Marines on a combat patrol sort through a massive amount of information to find and stop a determined attacker—a process that involves constant observation and orientation—Van Horne and Riley saw the advantage of refining the curriculum from the training program and developed it for a civilian audience.

The Marines describe six human behavioral domains people should learn, understand, and continuously evaluate to increase their situational awareness and personal safety.[6] Beyond the value of detecting a potential threat, knowing these six domains—*kinesics*, *biometric cues*, *proxemics*, *geographics*, *iconography*, and *atmospherics*—helps us develop a typology of what it means to be mindful in a research context. Our goal is not to conduct combat patrols so we can prevent attacks; we simply want to do our research safely. To do so, we will study these three aspects of situational awareness: people watching (*kinesics* and *biometric cues*), how people use space (*proxemics* and *geographics*), and knowing our surroundings (*iconography* and *atmospherics*).

People Watching: Kinesics and Biometric Cues

Although neurologists, biologists, and linguists have heated debates on the origins and evolution of speech development, most theories suggest that between 2 million and 500,000 years ago, humans first communicated in spoken words.[7] Before that, body language and guttural throat noises were the main forms of conveying emotions and feelings. Not much has changed since our evolutionary past; only 7 percent of a message's in-person impact involves the verbal presentation.[8] The rest is voice tone and body language.

Since Charles Darwin's 1872 study, *The Expressions of Emotion in Man and Animals*, researchers have recorded over one million nonverbal cues and signals.[9] This represents the first of Van Horne and Riley's domains, *kinesics*, which is a technical term for the study of body language.[10] Picking up these signals is often called common sense, but intuiting conscious and subconscious cues can be improved with learning and practice. For field researchers, studying kinesics does more than increase awareness. Employing and interpreting body language is a necessary skill for interviewing—a key component of any project, which I'll discuss in a later chapter.

As a skill, kinesics can be both simple and challenging to acquire. The basics are not all that difficult to grasp. As you consciously learn to read and recognize how body language works, you realize the breadth and scope of communication you routinely send and respond to. These observations start to seep into your subconscious, which makes you a better communicator in any language (spoken or not) and more aware of how your communication patterns are evolving in a conversation. Specific gestures might mean more or less than the experts say, and your conscious mind can often be the most difficult place to read body language.[11] You will really know you are reading body language accurately when you aren't thinking about it at all.[12]

Interpreting kinesics is a holistic exercise. First, although individual signals provide clues and perspective, a person's crossed legs or open palms, for example, are only part of an overall *cluster* of a person's nonverbal presentation, defined as a grouping of three or more points of nonverbal communication.[13] The more time you spend with someone, the higher level of *congruence* you'll be able to determine in his or her movements, meaning whether or not you have seen people respond with similar gestures before.[14] Finally, reading body language is most effective when placed in the *context* of a given cultural or physical situation, which enables more accurate pattern recognition.[15]

For example, unlike head gestures, which are mostly identical across cultures—the head shake "no" is common across the planet and is thought to have evolved from prehistoric infants rejecting their mother's milk when full—hand and arm gestures are often culturally specific.[16] Depending on the country, extended fingers and thumbs from one or both hands could be positive, neutral, or obscene. In 1985, five University of Texas fans from the United States were arrested outside the Vatican for causing a public disturbance; they had been walking through city streets throughout the country waving the "hook 'em" sign: an index and pinky finger extended from a fist.[17] In Italy, the gesture means your spouse is cheating on you.

Palm displays are more common signals across cultures. Open palms, which are common in Southern European and Latin American nonverbal communication, indicate submission and sincerity; exposing the vulnerable wrist interior is another way of saying "I have no hidden agenda, and I am offering myself to your fate."[18] The closed palm, in contrast, symbolizes authority and concealment. Picture the Sphinx sitting atop his throne, hands clamped down, or imagine a meeting with a supervisor sitting with folded hands.[19] Americans often mix open and closed palm gestures in an "even handed" manner when speaking, in keeping with a culture that emphasizes notions of equality and egalitarianism. Palm gestures are least common in Asia, particularly in business meetings. In Japan, arms are typically kept under the table during negotiations, which can feel unsettling for those who enter unprepared.

How can you pick out a seated American in an international airport? Watch how their legs are crossed. Only American men (and some women) cross legs in the dominant "figure four" style of foot placed on opposite knee, crotch exposed. This thrusts the pelvis forward, exerting subliminal possession over a territorial sphere, and presents the shoe or foot sole to whoever is seated adjacent, which is offensive across the Middle East and North Africa. Combine this pose with clasping hands behind head and leaning back, and it becomes a classic American power pose—the seated cowboy, confident and dominant in their imagined realm.[20]

Knowing universal foot gestures is useful not just for travel but also when standing in cocktail parties or post-meeting conversations. During pauses when meeting new people, take a quick glance down at their feet. People naturally point one or both feet toward persons or objects of interest. If someone is talking to you with one foot pointed away, they have only halfhearted engagement in the discussion. Foot indicators are less useful in common areas like public transportation or other spaces where people point feet as accommodations require.[21]

Biometric cues are a type of body language that also involves physical responses, but these are more deliberate, uncontrollable, and automatic than kinesics.[22] Pupils dilate involuntarily when a person feels stimulated or afraid. Blinking rates increase under stress, and moisture is drawn away from extremities, leaving anxious people pale and with "dry mouth."[23] In an otherwise normal environment, noticing people with these cues could indicate a threat you haven't observed, or it could mean your presence, for whatever reason, has caused discomfort. In an interview, these indicators are warning signs that you have stumbled on a sensitive topic and should move forward cautiously.

Facial body language, and the biometric cues it reveals, is what people instinctively read and interpret. In conversation with someone, we are naturally drawn to eye contact even when we don't understand another person's spoken language. How do you intuitively tell if a smile is sincere? Your peripheral vision notices whether or not wrinkles have appeared next to the eyes. If the crow's feet aren't present, the smile is defensive. Likewise, pupil dilation is a biometric cue that automatically reveals interest or defensiveness; when people feel hesitant the pupils get small and narrow, but excitement and interest widen the dark circles.[24]

Studying body language and learning biometric cues are not magic tricks or panaceas. These skills do not simplify every encounter or remove the need for spoken words to get things done. What learning body language does is increase the capacity for unconscious learning and reacting, which makes you a more comfortable, confident, and situationally aware field researcher. By taking time to watch how people communicate nonverbally, you'll feel better trusting your instincts even when you can't understand the words.

How People Use Space: Proxemics and Geographics
As you develop your skills in watching what people say to each other nonverbally, two more aspects of situational awareness involve how people interact spatially. Studying proxemics, or the interaction between people and how they use the space around them, enables a field researcher to

analyze group dynamics by observing movement and personal distance.[25] And watching *geographics*, or the way people relate to their physical environment, tells a field researcher who controls access to and from a certain space.[26]

Proxemics defines intimate, personal, social, and public zones of personal space. Movement from a social area and into someone's personal space indicates mutual familiarity and mutual permission to share space. Movement away from someone's personal zone and into social or public space indicates reactions of either attraction or revulsion from an individual or group. When in a public area, people generally move toward things they like and away from things they want to avoid. In a public zone, people who know each other well stand together, thus forming their own "personal zone" within a social or public space.[27]

We need look no further than school playgrounds, workplace cafeterias, and cocktail parties to see how proxemics relates to situational awareness. For field researchers, watching proxemics in a group enables an observer to understand the social dynamics present in the space. When sitting down for a group interview, a researcher may notice someone leaning into a supposed authority figure's personal space. Even though the other person isn't speaking, the "leader" keeps turning toward them deferentially. Proxemics may suggest the actual leader is using someone junior as a proxy because the interviewer hasn't yet gained the leader's trust.

Once, I sat down in an abandoned building in Amsterdam that 126 men and women had occupied for five months. The Netherlands had denied their asylum claims, and the building had been the only place where they could survive the winter. As I sat and ate with a group in a makeshift living room, I talked with an elderly woman rolling cigarettes. When she warmed up to my presence, other younger men began to do the same, demonstrating interest by moving toward me and turning in my direction to talk. Although she was not presented as a person of authority, proxemic responses affirmed her influence in the group.

Geographics involves watching how people act in a place by themselves. Generally, people move with confidence in a familiar area and cautiously in a new place. If people are anchored to a certain space, they feel safe coming and going as they please, without any restrictions. In their own way, homes, office buildings, conference areas, and restaurant tables have as exclusive a requirement for invitation as a VIP section in a nightclub. Situational awareness increases not only by knowing who has permission to freely access a geographic space—rooms, buildings, streets, neighborhoods, cities, or countries—but by discerning who controls admission into a space. [28]

Beyond increasing situational awareness, studying how people act in public and personal space also assists field researchers with personal security planning. Knowing who has the ability to enter the room where you are living and sleeping could indicate whether or not hired staff or building owners have the ability or intent to violate your privacy. Reducing the number of people with access to your quarters, as well as friendliness and courtesy to landlords and employees, are both useful security techniques grounded in proxemics, geographics, and common sense. Acknowledging that you may not be able to control who enters and exits your space enlists others in your goal of keeping you and your belongings safe.

Knowing Your Surroundings:
Iconography and Atmospherics

Watching how people behave, react to one another, or move through the spaces they occupy are all techniques that increase a field researcher's attentiveness toward how others are reacting to the researcher's presence. The final two clues are in paying attention to the environment itself. This includes *iconography*, or visual language, that is present in a new place as well as the *atmospherics*, or collective energy, existing in a particular location. [29]

Iconography allows a field researcher to note important symbols that identify both personal attachments and local affiliations. Graffiti, posters, flags, pins, banners, signs, bumper stickers, tattoos, and clothing are among the most common means of iconographic messaging. [30] Public iconography, such as flag displays, religious symbols, or graffiti tags, can provide clues about regional identification of allegiance, belief, or ownership. Personal iconography, such as tattoos, clothing, or visible paraphernalia in a work office, tells a researcher what an interviewee believes or wants others around them to think is most important.

One of my assignments during a research project in the Baltic states included comparing and contrasting the Estonian and Latvian land borders with Russia. As part of the project, I needed to determine the national sympathies of Russian-speaking people living close to the border. In communities along Latvia's border with Russia, approximately one of every twelve houses flew or displayed Latvia's national flag. In Narva, the major Estonian city on the Russia border, few, if any, homes displayed the Estonian flag. Iconography suggested national identity was a different type of motivating force with Russian speakers in Latvia's border region than in eastern Estonia, which offered context for follow-up questions with interviewees in both countries.[31]

For a research project in Senegal, a different form of local iconography increased my situational awareness. After three days of taking taxis around the capital city of Dakar, I noticed a sticker depicting an imam prominently displayed on the dashboard. The local religious leader was based in Mali, and his passionate sermons opposing violence and embracing peace had won him followers throughout the region. Had I not noticed the recurring picture, I would not have been able to enjoy a conversation about it with the taxi driver, who explained the imam's significance.

Combining iconography with observations about people and spaces leads a researcher to consider atmospherics: the collective energy, mood, or feel of a situation or place. This is not a mystical thing; the group emotions of euphoria at a sports event or political rally are as specific, coherent, and tangible as collective grief following a terrorist attack or natural disaster.[32] The phenomenon might best be explained as an environmental, public, and group sensation combining the five previous situational awareness components. Noise levels, social activity, and the general feeling of order or chaos play a role in atmospheric determination.

Field researchers can gain an edge in their work by identifying the normal atmospheric state in a particular environment as quickly as possible. By understanding what is routine, you can identify your own "new normal" as you assimilate. This makes you more aware of any deviations from what is standard—such as noise when silence is normal, or vice versa. As previously mentioned, slowing down is the most important first step to determining what is normal. Avoid talking on your mobile phone in public as much as possible—especially when walking around. Conversations distract from your ability to observe your new environment, which not only reduces your ability to identify and avoid threats but also inhibits basic research.

Soon after arriving in Afghanistan, a friend of mine was talking on her cell in Kabul to get directions to a meeting place. She had been in the city for several weeks but had not walked through this particular neighborhood. She was distracted while talking on her mobile and was not able to notice she was being watched. Moments later, a man snatched her phone out of her hand before she noticed his presence, and he threatened to attack her. She emerged unscathed but learned a practical lesson on the costs of reducing awareness.

Moving beyond Fear, and Fitting In

The most common fear I hear discussed from first-time international travelers—and what often prompts a conversation about situational awareness in the first place—is about staying safe. How will I do my work and go about daily living? How do I protect myself against terrorist attacks, pickpockets, scam artists, or even people wanting to harm me because of my research interests? How do I form these new field habits while I still feel afraid of the unknown?

There's nothing wrong with fear. It is just as real an emotion as happiness, and monitoring it, either in or out of the field, is important. Sometimes fear's presence is a good sign; it means we're moving beyond our comfort zone and need to stay steady. Other times, fear tells us to pay attention; instincts say not to walk down a certain alley, and something we can't explain urges caution. Although knowing and using fear is as much a part of the field research process as it is with any human experience, most fears are likely to be unfounded when sorting out the nervousness associated with travel.[33]

When cautiously alert, conscious of one's environment, and aware of one's relationship to people and spaces, field researchers are more likely to find themselves feeling comfortable much sooner in a new place. Whether your assignment is for one week or several years, assimilation is what a field researcher hopes to achieve. Studying situational awareness does not automatically mean you will blend in. As with all lessons in this handbook, personal application is the primary difference in how prepared and confident you feel with entering into a new environment.

Being situationally aware does not automatically guarantee anyone's safety. But greater observation skills that come from studying the six behavioral domains enable faster and more effective orientation in any new place. While this may (or may not) mean your instincts will react more quickly if a threat emerges, learning to perceive people and survey spaces is one of the most pleasurable skills in the entire field research experience. As your awareness increases, you will be able to sit for hours at a restaurant, park bench, or café. And as you watch, and occasionally jot down notes, you will be reading your new surroundings and the people living in them like a book you can't put down.

Key Points

- Situational awareness is a rational, sustained synthesis of instinct and observation—a fusion of cognitive feedback and intangible "feel."

- Seen through the Boyd Loop framework, situational awareness is about the first two components of the loop: observation and orientation. Observation is paying attention to your surroundings. Orientation involves identifying choices and available options.
- The six behavioral domains of situational awareness are *kinesics*, *biometric cues*, *proxemics*, *geographics*, *iconography*, and *atmospherics*.
- Only 7 percent of a message's impact from one human to another comes from verbal communication. The rest is from voice tone and body language.
- The three techniques to remember and apply when reading and interpreting kinesics, or body language, are *clustering*, *congruence*, and *context*.
- Biometric cues are a type of body language that also involves physical responses, but these are more deliberate, uncontrollable, and automatic than kinesics.
- Proxemics defines intimate, personal, social, and public zones of personal space. People generally move toward things they like and away from things they want to avoid.
- Geographics is watching how people act in a place by themselves. Generally, people move with confidence in a familiar area. In a new place, most move cautiously.
- Iconography, or visual language, allows a field researcher to note important symbols that identify both personal attachments and local affiliations.
- Atmospherics is the collective energy, mood, or feel of a situation or place. It combines the information from the five other domains with noise levels, social activity, and the general feeling of order or chaos.
- Field researchers should identify the normal state of affairs in their new research environment as quickly as possible. By understanding what is routine, you can also identify your own "new normal" as you assimilate.

Notes

1. Because "situational awareness" has military origins, the definitions used in different doctrinal publications vary from simplistic ("knowing what is going on around you") to excessive ("the perception of environmental elements with respect to time and space"). My definition of the term is informed by Boyd's *Left of Bang* and de Becker's *The Gift of Fear*, but mostly by my own fieldwork and Marine Corps experience.

2. Brett McKay, "How to Develop the Situational Awareness of Jason Bourne," *The Art of Manliness* (blog), February 5, 2015, http://www.artofmanliness.com/2015/02/05/how-to-develop-the-situational-awareness-of-jason-bourne/.

3. John Boyd, "Destruction and Creation," paper, September 3, 1976, http://www.goalsys.com/books/documents/DESTRUCTION_AND_CREATION.pdf.

4. Ibid.

5. Patrick Van Horne and Jason Riley, *Left of Bang: How the Marine Corps' Combat Hunter Program Can Save Your Life* (New York: Black Irish Books, 2014), 65–69.

6. Ibid., 65–66.

7. Allan Pease and Barbara Pease, *The Definitive Book of Body Language* (London: Orion, 2004), 8.

8. Ibid., 9.

9. Ibid.

10. Van Horne and Riley, *Left of Bang*, 70.

11. John Baldoni, "7 Surprising Truths about Body Language," *Forbes*, October 25, 2012, http://www.forbes.com/sites/nickmorgan/2012/10/25/7-surprising-truths-about-body-language/#52eaf96b2987.

12. Ibid.

13. Pease and Pease, *Definitive Book of Body Language*, 21–22.

14. Ibid., 23–24.

15. Ibid., 25.

16. Ibid., 232.

17. Ibid., 124.

18. Ibid., 31–39.

19. Ibid.

20. Ibid., 209–28.

21. Ibid.

22. Van Horne and Riley, *Left of Bang*, 94–97.

23. Ibid., 99–101.

24. Ibid.

25. Ibid., 106.

26. Ibid., 115.

27. Ibid., 106–16.

28. Ibid., 117–30.

29. Ibid., 117–32.

30. Ibid., 130–38.

31. A colleague and I took surveys that later proved our thesis. Most Narva residents do not even speak Estonian, while Russian speakers in Latvia identified with both Russian and Latvian nationalism. The iconography accurately reflected public sentiment.

32. Van Horne and Riley, *Left of Bang*, 139–47.

33. For a detailed discussion of this phenomena, see Gavin de Becker's *The Gift of Fear*.

Research Preparation
Review Questions

Chapter 1: Framing the "Other"
- Why is field research important? What can be gained from going into the field that cannot be found from online research or video interviews?
- Is field research an art or a science? Explain your answer.
- How does field research sequence into an overall problem-solving context? Is it the first phase or the last? Explain.
- What is a useful first step in fieldwork preparation?
- What are examples of natural bias? Why is the issue of bias important for a field researcher to consider?
- Who are the Nacirema? Why do they matter?
- What is the "Other"? Why does the concept of "Othering" matter to a field researcher?
- How can a field researcher learn to identify and shed bias?

Chapter 2: Developing Your Research Style
- What is positionality? How does this idea interact with developing our own individual research styles?
- Compare and contrast academic, government, and corporate researchers. In what ways are they the same? How are they different?
- What types of predispositions are academic field researchers prone to? What about corporate or government field researchers?
- What is a research style? What variables affect it?
- How do researchers begin developing their style? Can this be accomplished before going into the field? Why or why not?
- Should a field researcher take notes? If so, how? Why is this important?

Chapter 3: Improving Situational Awareness

- What is situational awareness? Why is it important? How does the concept of situational awareness relate to the Boyd Loop?
- What are the six behavioral domains of situational awareness?
- How much communication takes place verbally versus nonverbally?
- What are three techniques to remember and apply when reading and interpreting kinesics, or body language?
- What are biometric cues? How are they different from kinesics?
- What are proxemics? How does this concept relate to personal space?
- In what way does geographics explain how people move around in places?
- How does studying iconography increase a field researcher's situational awareness?
- How does the concept of atmospherics relate to the other situational awareness domains?
- Why is it important for field researchers to identify the normal state of affairs quickly in their new research environment?

PART II
The Field

4

Logistics and Networking

In 2015, I completed a field research project for a client that required a detailed assessment along several international borders in Europe. Originally, I had planned to use public ground transportation to access the areas and then canvas most of the terrain on foot. But as part of my research planning, I also looked into rental car options, locations, and availability.

Once my research partner and I got on the ground, both the research objective and transportation knowledge had changed. The bus network was slower than we had anticipated, and having independent mobility would consequently be a much better option. We also had less time available to accomplish the research than we had thought we would have. We changed our plan, rented a car, and completed the border research in half the time originally scheduled. The car rental was more expensive, but, in this case, the budget was not as important as fulfilling the client's requirements.

As with field research in general, a deliberate yet flexible approach to logistics and networking yields the best results. Events change. Schedules shift. As it turns out, the bus network in Mexico is as efficient as the train system in Germany. Shared minivan taxis in Africa and the Middle East make it easier to meet and talk with new people. Sometimes flying from one place to another will get you between destinations faster but in a much less interesting way.

On the one hand, embracing the idea that you don't know what you don't know is a necessary part of the field research process—that is why you are going in the first place. But departing for the field without having done any preparation whatsoever is foolhardy, arrogant, and reckless. Itineraries and schedules should never be fixed in stone prior to any field research project. But they should exist. Field research demands flexibility but abhors ignorance.

This chapter will cover, at a general level, basic considerations on travel logistics and network planning for field researchers. Whatever plans you make are less important than the process you go through while making them. Plans themselves should remain fluid, but the act of planning will show you what transportation, lodging, security, and networking variables are going to impact your ability to complete your research.[1]

At first, this material might seem similar to information you might find in tourist guidebooks. Although certain aspects are alike, there are also important distinctions between research and tourism. Field researchers have a job to do. It is an interesting occupation, but it's still your craft and trade. There is a reason you're in the field, and that means data needs collecting, assignments need completing, articles need writing, and deliverables need delivering. Someone paid you to get them a product. Your task is to find it.

Getting to the Field

Once you know where you are going, you must decide how you're going to get there. To legally travel internationally, you will need a passport and possibly—depending on your country of origin and research destination—a visa. To get one, you will most likely need to send your passport to a visa agency or local consulate along with additional forms. Planning your field research so you can avoid violating policy by checking on these requirements ahead of time will go a long way toward making your research productive and incident free.

Unless you're traveling exclusively by ground and/or ship to your field research destination, your next step is most likely an airline ticket purchase. Some of the discount methods and cost variables include one-way ticket purchases, open-ended travel through partner airline package purchases, and off-season travel ticketing. Point deals accumulated through frequent flyer memberships can often yield cheap fares, while peak season travel and limited flight options increase costs.

Even if a travel agency is booking your flights, the agent will most likely want to know what flight options you prefer. Just as with domestic airline travel in the US, international airline travel uses central regional hub airports as primary transit points. These hubs are connected through international airline partner alliances, which are networks of airlines that offer benefits to connect passengers through cooperation and mutual frequent-flyer-point accumulation within the network. As of 2016, the three largest international airline networks are Star Alliance (twenty-eight airlines), SkyTeam (twenty), and OneWorld (fifteen). If you know the region where you're traveling to, there may be better travel options from one of the airline networks, which might drive decisions about everything from discount options to frequent flyer mileage accumulation.[2]

Living in the Field

If you're on a budget, air travel is the highest priority item to price and decide, particularly if the research assignment will take you into the field for only a month or less. The next most important item is choosing where you will live while you work. Will you pick a single location to use as a base while traveling during the day for research and interviews? Or will your fieldwork require greater mobility, compelling you to shift from one place to another at regular intervals? Is your assignment open-ended, or do you have time constraints? Do you get to decide where you will live while in the field, or does your program manager, research supervisor, corporate policy director, or higher headquarters make the decision for you?

If you have a choice, consider staying in a nice hotel on at least two occasions: the night you arrive in the field and the night prior to returning home. After processing through customs and stumbling sleep deprived into a new time zone, it is well worth paying slightly too much for a taxi to take you somewhere comfortable so you have an evening to rest, shower, and sleep. Wherever you are, you'll be able to get your bearings and get around much better the next day. And it will be your way of rewarding yourself for a job well done on the way out.

If you'll be basing out of a single location for several weeks in the field, an apartment, room, or house rental may prove the best option. The best-known worldwide services, which include Airbnb, Homeaway.com, and Sabbaticalhomes.com, connect short-term renters with available quarters at local rates. As with most services, longer stays provide the landlord with a higher income stream, which yields cheaper rates for renters. Hundreds, if not thousands, of short-term rental websites exist worldwide, and whatever region you are traveling to may have an array of local options that can be found only through direct internet searches.

If you are a freelance field researcher with time and interest, consider a work-for-lodging exchange to fund your project. Workaway.info connects hosts with boarders who volunteer time and energy on farms, vineyards, ranches, and other seasonal homesteads worldwide. Stay open to changing your situation once you get on the ground. The best opportunities available are often negotiated in person, and thinking through

multiple solutions provides a field researcher with options for lodging
and for comparing and contrasting the type of research prospects each
arrangement might offer.[3]

Although long-term housing can provide ease of movement and local
contacts, there are potential disadvantages to staying in the same place
for several weeks or months. You may not be exposed to an adequate
variety of environments for the data you are collecting as you would if you
were staying in multiple locations. If you are doing sensitive research,
you might find yourself open to personal security vulnerabilities; the
longer you stay in one place, the more people can learn and report on
your movements and whereabouts.

If your research has to be done in multiple locations, and you already
have local contacts, stay somewhere cheap and close to your expected
meeting sites. If your "base" is changing every three days or less, hotel
stays may be necessary to better accommodate the demands of flexibility.
And if you know you're going to be traveling around, it becomes that much
more important to dedicate a day or two where you have nothing scheduled, just so you can explore.

Working in the Field

It is valuable to plan ahead at some level for the moments you set aside
for walking around the city, for getting lost, for taking local minibus taxis
to places that aren't on the map, just to see where they go. Multiple field
research locations require more detailed logistics planning; these projects will benefit from building a basic itinerary on paper before getting
on the ground (see appendix B). This level of front-end planning is less
critical if you're staying in one place for a long time but essential if you're
migrating through multiple locations every few days with the intention of
collecting as much information and data as possible.

Once you have a basic idea of where you're going and how you'll get
there, it's time to make sure you stay as healthy as possible while you're
researching. Healthy does not mean avoiding all physical discomfort;
erratic sleep patterns and episodic traveler's diarrhea are inevitable for
every researcher. Healthy, in this context, means not contracting a deadly
or incapacitating disease.

In 1971, the World Health Organization (WHO) published a standard
International Certificate of Vaccination; copies are publicly available in
small, tan booklets. Get one, and have a medical professional check your
records and transcribe all of the vaccinations you've ever received. Re-

gardless of where you're going, you will probably need a booster shot or two and something you hadn't expected. Get them. It's important.

In some countries, you'll have to show proof of vaccination from a specific disease as an entry requirement. As an example, several West African countries mandate proof of yellow fever vaccination for entrance; regional immigration officials look for a stamped physician's signature in your WHO booklet as rigorously as they check for a visa before permitting entry.

Once you've got your vaccinations, assess your own personal health condition. How much risk are you comfortable assuming? What types of medications do you normally use for common ailments like colds, headaches, nausea, and fever? Will you need condoms or birth control? Will you need tampons, and does the country where you are going sell them? (In some countries, only pads are sold.) Everyone has a health routine, and there's no reason to disrupt it abroad. If you take aspirin or ginseng or mint tea to cure your troubles, have a stash available.

Buy or assemble a small first-aid kit that suits your field research destination: Band-Aids, Neosporin, hydrocortisone, medical tape, and a gauze wrap or two will normally be good enough to start you out. Also, remember many medications can be purchased in other countries besides the United States, often at much lower cost. Malaria pills are one example among many, and buying them in your new locale illustrates just one of the many ways a daily task can become part of your field research. We will talk more about how to handle eating and drinking in the next chapter—there is usually much less to worry about than you might think.

A Field Researcher's Gear List

What should you pack? Take one "office bag" for your laptop, notebooks, recording devices, and other gear. And take one "personal bag" for clothes, coats, and shoes. One of them should be a shoulder-carry bag and the other a backpack. Avoid roller luggage; it is difficult to maneuver, especially on and off a train, bus, or taxi. Pack at least a week's worth of season-appropriate clothes along with extra socks and underwear. Have at least one nice outfit for interviews and at least one rugged outfit for getting dirty.

The rest of your kit should be as much of what you could wear in any environment along the spectrum of what your research might require. Do your own laundry every few days. And above all, don't overpack. Overpacking means taking more into the field than you can carry on your person. You should always be able to carry all your stuff yourself. Take as little as possible; you can buy anything else you need once you arrive.

Financial Planning

What about money? First, look up the local currency and exchange rate, both with dollars and also with euros or another major regional currency. Memorize these before departing as a baseline, and then double-check it again as soon as you arrive since rates change daily. If you're traveling for corporate or government fieldwork, examine local credit and debit card policies with your organization's financial office.

Make sure you know your balance limits and purchase restrictions (if any) on your credit card ahead of time. Know the expense report and invoicing process before you leave; many researchers have found themselves carrying credit card balances for thousands of dollars because they didn't understand how their organization would pay them back and failed to send in the right paperwork when they completed the project.

ATMs are common worldwide and are generally safe to use for cash withdrawals in most countries (Nigeria, the global epicenter of financial scams, is a notable exception). Unless absolutely needed, avoid currency exchange houses whenever possible, especially at airports or expensive hotels—the exchange rates will be horrible. Carry at least $200 in cash, initially in a mix of dollars and euros or another common international currency. Carry as much as is practical in local currency and then plan to spend it before you leave.

If managing your own budget, submit a travel notification for the countries you'll be visiting with your bank or credit union, either on their website or with a phone call. This will ensure your credit card transactions aren't blocked as a fraud-prevention measure.

For some strange reason, many travelers decide to carry cash and credit cards in money belts, special pouches, fanny or belly packs, or other odd ways that are completely different from the methods they use for carrying valuables at home. This is not necessary or smart. There is no good reason for travelers to carry cash or credit cards any differently abroad than at home.

Since I was a teenager, I have carried money and credit cards in my front trouser pocket. I've found this safer and more practical than a back-pocket carry because it is much easier for me to use peripheral vision to see if someone is attempting to reach for my front pockets than the back ones. I do the same thing wherever I go. The only exception I make when traveling might be separating larger cash stashes into luggage or a personal cache. Examples would include carrying your daily cash in a wallet, money clip, billfold, or purse and then putting a cash stash in a sock (or for women, bra), locked safe, or hidden luggage compartment.

Whatever carrying method works for you at home is the same one you should employ when in the field. Getting fancy with fanny packs reduces your ability to pay attention to your main tasks: analyzing your new surroundings, taking notes on your observations and experiences, and making sure you're remaining aware of your new environment.

Emergency Management

What about emergencies out of your control? Natural disasters? Terrorist attacks? Kidnappings? You have several options. There are many schools of thought on travel insurance. If your research destination will take you into remote areas, you may want to consider short-term medical evacuation insurance, which would cover an emergency evacuation to a hospital covered by your health insurance. Most travel insurance plans are long on both specifics and loopholes, so be certain you understand exactly what you're buying and what it covers, depending on your situation and research objectives.

The need to have emergency points of contact—located both at home and in the field—varies from situation to situation. Look up, learn, and discuss your organization or client's emergency management policies before departing. If you are a solo researcher and not carrying a mobile phone—unlikely, but still possible—maintain a standard practice of checking an email account at a set frequency, particularly if you cannot connect daily. Global communications capabilities mean loved ones will worry if this activity is interrupted, particularly if they hear of any disturbing news happening anywhere near your travel area. Ultimately, this is a personal variable and is driven by each individual's situation, preference, and risk tolerance.

Professional Specific Logistics

If you're on a corporate or government research assignment, then you may need to purchase certain types of tickets that cost more but have more flexible options if your itinerary changes. Corporate and government researchers are usually required to make arrangements through a travel agency (yes, even in the internet age travel agencies still exist).

Academic field researchers and freelance journalists usually buy their own tickets. Although you will likely be looking for the cheapest fare possible, you will also have other variables to consider when purchasing tickets that depend on your field research purpose. If you are traveling for academic field research or independent journalism, it is useful to budget more for airline tickets than required. Even if airline travel costs have been factored into your travel budget, airport, website, and service fees can often add up.

As a corporate or government field researcher, many of your logistics and networking activities might be handled on your behalf. But when possible, don't leave these important elements to others. Government officials—diplomats in particular—can find themselves living in an illusory logistics bubble that reduces atmospheric awareness and common sense. Having agencies or employees make reservations or schedule meetings is sometimes necessary, but when this happens to you, the mental distractions of telling other people what to do weaken you in two ways. First, you lose the ability to observe your environment because your day-to-day success doesn't depend on knowing it. Second, and more importantly, you won't know how to handle any problem—from routine disruptions to major crises—without calling someone else.

I saw this firsthand in February 2010 while returning to Washington, DC, from an assignment in Algeria. Winter weather delays had stranded all US-bound flights in Frankfurt, and a senior US State Department official—who would later become an ambassador—was furious and dismayed. While I stood in line, rebooked a later ticket, and snagged one of the last available hotel rooms, the official made frantic calls to various assistants and travel agents, growing increasingly displeased at everyone's collective inability to overcome the weather. I held a hotel room for the official out of sympathy and spent the next two days as an impromptu staffer. This person was so used to others telling them where to be and what to do that they seemed to have forgotten how to accomplish basic logistics without a concierge or aide.

Networking

Let's review. You know—or at least have a general idea—where you're going, how you're getting there, how you'll stay healthy, what you'll be packing, and how to handle emergencies. But before you get on the ground, you'd like to know—or at least have some sense of—who you'll be talking to. How do you start building a network in a place you've never been?

Begin with who you know at home. Start weeks in advance or as soon as you know you will be traveling. Ask friends and colleagues about their personal networks. Sort through that stack of business cards in your desk drawer or file cabinet and look for old acquaintances. You're not necessarily searching for someone to interview, just looking for a point of contact—like a rock climber hunting for a foot or hand hold to get to the next level.

Next, look through your online network. Find out how many degrees of separation you are from someone you'd like to talk with on Facebook, Twitter, or LinkedIn. Think about the industry of the people you'll be researching and look up related organizations, institutions, or officials. Cast a wide net and don't be afraid of reaching out to people you don't know. When taking the first steps to build your network, less is more. As mentioned before, the goal is to make an initial connection, not to disclose everything there is to know about your project or secure a full interview on the first request. Once you have one meeting set with a contact, ask if there's anyone else he or she recommends you meet with while you're in the area.

As you repeat this pattern and your network expands, consider the constraints on perspectives that may emerge as a result of how you and your trusted contacts have identified potential interviewees. Just as you have your own bias, so also will everyone whom you meet on the ground. As you transition from preparation into field research, take note of the background your interviewees are likely to bring into conversations. Remember, positionality is neither good nor bad, simply a research variable. Your interview experience may be either similar to or very different from your initial assumptions.

One administrative note for academic field researchers: almost all academic research abroad goes through some type of approval process to an academic board. In the United States this is called the Institutional Review Board. It has been a legal requirement for accredited research since 1964, when the 18th World Medical Assembly in Helsinki, Finland, called for adopting such a board following discussions of unethical research conduct at the International Military Tribunal of Nazi Germany.[4]

With this requirement in mind, the initial stage of network building is not necessarily the proper time for academic researchers to complete the Institutional Review Board checklist for interview requirements that, from an institutional perspective, took so long to get put in place and approved. Social science field researchers occasionally struggle with deciding when they should disclose their research objectives, complete necessary forms, and discuss privacy of data collection with potential interviewees. There will be time later to fulfill all of these formal requirements. For now, just focus on getting your foot in the door.

As with the entire process of field research, logistics and networking are both an art and science. The skills are not difficult to learn, and much of your planning will involve prescribed professional requirements and/or disciplined internet searches. With experience, you will become comfortable and confident with how logistics and networking variables impact one another. When meeting opportunities unfold and personal schedules change, your logistics will shift a bit. This is a normal part of the field research process. Get used to it—there will be even more changes once you get on the ground.

Key Points

- Professional field research demands flexibility but also requires detailed planning. While few things will not change, basic itineraries and schedules are still necessary.
- Fieldwork itineraries will likely look different from tourist schedules and should be developed based on your organization or client's required deliverables.
- Have a passport in hand before booking international travel. Know the visa requirements, if any, for the country or countries you will be visiting and your expected length of stay.
- The three largest international airline partner networks are Star Alliance, SkyTeam, and OneWorld. Use the same international airline network, and its hub airports, when booking airline travel as much as possible.
- Use an online fare as a baseline to search other options. Breaking up a single airline ticket with ground transportation or budget airlines can often result in a cheaper itinerary.
- If you have a choice, plan to stay in a nice hotel on two occasions: the night you arrive in the field and the night prior to returning home.
- Apartment, room, house rentals, or work-for-lodging options may prove better than hotel stays if you will be in a single location. If you are traveling often from one location to another—every three days or less—hotels may be a more practical choice.
- Have a medical professional check and transcribe your vaccinations into a WHO International Certificate of Vaccination booklet. Get vaccinations as necessary.

- Take one "office bag" and one "personal bag" for your gear. Use a shoulder-carry bag for one and a backpack for the other, as you prefer. Avoid roller luggage when possible.
- ATMs are common worldwide. Unless absolutely necessary, avoid currency exchange houses. Carry cash and credit cards in the field the same way you do at home.
- When building your initial field network, think about the industry you will be researching and look up related organizations, institutions, officials, and personnel.
- Less is more. The goal as you build your network is to make initial connections, not to tell them everything about your project or secure a full interview on the first request.

Notes

1. Planning for field time is a highly personal process. Observations, thoughts, and anecdotes on logistics planning and networking preparation are drawn from my own field research experience and anecdotal conversations with other professional researchers of different backgrounds and experiences.
2. Edward Hasbrouck, *The Practical Nomad: How to Travel around the World* (Emeryville: Avalon, 2011), 152–202.
3. Ibid., 559–68.
4. "Institutional Review Board Guidebook," US Department of Health and Human Services, 1993, accessed February 7, 2016, www.hhs.gov.

5

On the Ground

The first flight is longer than you would like it to be but not as exhausting as you had feared. Cabins are pressurized at an oxygen level around 6,000 feet, so you eat the meals, drink the water, decline the alcohol, and enjoy the movies. You get up, stretch, and walk around when you can.

You are still tired when you stumble into the customs line at the transfer airport. You hand over your passport, which is promptly stamped and returned for transit. You snake through the duty-free shops and stop to use the restroom. The airport is large, loud, and busy. Everyone is on their way to somewhere else.

Your next flight is shorter; you start by reading an airline magazine but end up watching something mindless in an effort to stay awake so your body clock can advance itself into the new time zone. As the airplane descends to your research destination, you look out the window, absorbing the view of the geography, scenery, and movement, occasionally snapping a picture or two with your mobile or digital camera.

The customs line upon arrival is not as long as the one was at transit, but the officer spends more time scrutinizing your passport and entry form. Your picture and fingerprints are digitally captured for biometric matching, a process that has become standard procedure at border crossings worldwide. You answer the questions honestly, courteously, and confidently, but without unnecessary elaboration—not a small achievement when you haven't slept for two days. There's no checked luggage for you to pick up at baggage claim; you've packed light just as you planned and walk through the green "nothing to declare" exit.

The arrival terminal is packed with people waiting expectantly and holding signs. Your fellow passengers are fumbling with their mobiles and pointing toward relatives. You stop at an ATM, withdraw a reasonable sum, and look for the taxi line. As you make your way toward it, someone approaches you offering a direct ride. You brush him away. Then someone else makes their way to you. Then someone else. You glance at the stagnant taxi line and decide to go with one of the hucksters. You know you'll pay more, but it will get you to the hotel faster. It's the first of many gut calls you'll make.

As the driver tells you about the city and his life, you practice saying courtesies—thank you, please, hello, goodbye—in the national language. He gives you a business card and tells you to call him anytime you need a ride. You've overpaid the fare but have made a contact and had a research encounter, what you might call an informal interview. You mentally note all the things that you'll need to write down once you are alone in your room.

You check in and chat with the hotel clerk. She is courteous and tells you about interesting things to see and good places to eat. You remember to ask for a walking map, not only because they are useful—you can never have enough maps—but because you can learn some things about an area from seeing which establishments have advertised to tourists on the maps that hotels commonly offer.

You get to your room, sit down, and dig out your notebook. After eating, drinking, and showering, you write down everything you've observed so far. This was a lot easier to do when you weren't exhausted, but you've trained yourself now into the habit of taking field notes. You know from practice that if you don't record your thoughts then you'll forget what you heard and said and thought and saw. You email your contact that you've arrived and confirm a late afternoon coffee meeting for tomorrow before going to bed.

———

Every field researcher feels a bit of shock the first time he or she goes to an unfamiliar place for a project or assignment. The initial moments may be tinged with fear and anticipation. For those with more life experience in moves or transitions, this sense of uncertainty may not feel as complicated. Field researchers can draw psychological context during these first few hours from parallel moments of other life changes.

The first day often sets a pattern for the first week, or, depending on your length of stay, for your entire trip. Pace yourself. You aren't at your best right now. If you are on a government assignment or part of a study abroad team, most of your initial logistics will already have been decided by someone else. If you've been set up in a hotel or are welcomed into a host family, be polite and courteous but don't do too much. The most important things after arriving are eating, showering/bathing, and sleeping. There will be plenty of time for everything else soon enough.

Dispatch the necessary texts, emails, or phone calls to let whoever needs to know that you've arrived safely. And by all means, capture any notes that your experience of the day requires. But don't spend your first night exploring. Your body needs to adjust to a new sleeping cycle, new food routine, new bacteria—all of the new environmental factors—as soon as possible. Resting and pacing yourself are just as necessary now as the idea of going to unknown places was before you began examining your own biases.

Regardless of whether your field research is for a corporate, academic, or government assignment, this scenario illustrates a typical first day. Team structure, task specifics, and expected length of stay are the most important variables that shift the patterns of orientation when starting in the field. For example, a four-person government research team assigned to investigate cybersecurity capabilities in Cyprus for eight days will have a busier first day than an academic field researcher who has eight weeks to complete dissertation research on a similar topic. More people usually means more tasks have to be accomplished over shorter stays, which usually results in busier itineraries. Since this inherently reduces a team's ability to accomplish the "slow travel" analysis we discussed earlier, research teams depend on networking with freelancers who can often go deeper, even though they take longer.

Solo field researchers who can build their own itineraries should, as much as possible, avoid making the first field visit an interview. Freelancers will benefit from making initial contact with someone on a friendly, collegial level. Whether or not they are part of formal research is irrelevant—the purpose for the first meeting is for you to get comfortable talking to the people who live in your new environment. Through casual conversation, any newcomer will naturally begin to mirror local body language—and as an astute field researcher who has prepared, studied, and practiced ahead of time, you will slowly, unconsciously, and effortlessly find yourself blending in.

Here we approach a common professional divide. Because government field research often occurs in teams, it may also come with scripted itineraries, which can be just as true for academics researching on a funded group trip. As we discussed in the previous chapter, itineraries may be out of a researcher's control. Being part of a research team with a tight sched-ule may have advantages. Important interviews may have been previously arranged, and other aspects of the trip may have been constructed for the specific purpose of collecting data.

The solo researcher has the benefits of flexibility and time when mak-ing adjustments to itinerary and interview choices. Setting one's own schedule means there is more opportunity for walking around and ori-enting to a new area. Meetings may not take place quickly, but when they happen, a solo researcher will be informed by observations that have taken place in a broader context than would have otherwise occurred. Consider how the following solo research activity could assist in prepar-ing with interviews and other data collection during a research trip.

––––––––––

You wake up at an odd time but fall back asleep, rising again just before the free breakfast buffet closes. Fortified with local food, you head out for a walk, asking the hotel for a late check-out as you depart. You get on and off a bus, mapping out a route to the apartment you found on Airbnb where you'll stay for the next three weeks. You board a different bus and end up far outside the city, away from the tourist areas in a neighbor-hood way off the map. You are lost. And that is excellent—because now you know you are lost in exactly the way you are supposed to be.

You walk and look and walk and look some more, taking pictures of storefronts and signage and graffiti. You buy a grilled sandwich from a street vendor, remembering the three cardinal rules of street vendor food purchases:

· Eat from stands where local people are eating
· Buy from vendors selling only one or two types of meals
· Make sure whatever you eat is cooked in front of you

You sit on a bench, eat, and take notes on your morning observations. You have some idea how to get to the café a few blocks from the hotel where you are supposed to meet a classmate's former study abroad sib-ling, but you aren't willing to chance missing the visit on your ignorance of the local bus route. You walk to a busy street, flag down a taxi, and take it back to the hotel. You check out of your room, stash your luggage in the storage closet that the hotel offers for outgoing guests, and make your way to the café.

The meeting is courteous, if inconclusive. Although your new friend does not know anyone who is connected to your research industry, he was familiar with several good restaurants and had useful tips on other places to go. Back at the hotel, you grab your gear and take the bus to your Airbnb rental. The spare apartment room has all the necessities: bed, shower, laundry, kitchen, desk, and Wi-Fi. You'll be fine staying here for the rest of your research trip.

You put your things away and find one of the restaurants your friend recommended. The waiter asks if you want bottled water, and you point to the tap instead. Yes, many people are paranoid about drinking the water in other countries, but you decide since you will be there for two weeks, you will get the local bacteria in your gut as soon as possible. An experienced field researcher gave you that tip: a day of bowel discomfort is better than enduring weeks of water paranoia. Once your intestines are acculturated, you can feel more comfortable with Anthony Bourdain–style eating and drinking. Most tap water is purified worldwide—to the point that many European and Asian countries warn their citizens not to drink water while traveling in the United States.

Two days after your first restaurant visit, you are on your way to your first interview. Through a LinkedIn connection, you are able to meet up with an official—she doesn't seem to speak your language any better than you do hers, but you feel comfortable hiring the college friend you met on the first day to translate. You use LinkedIn to research other industry associations as well. At first, the staff you contact doesn't respond, but you eventually find an association representative who will welcome you for a visit.

At the first interview, your friend's translations were slow and choppy. It made the interview so difficult to follow that the official eventually switched to hand gestures with drawings on a white board. Although it went well overall, you decide you will leave your friend behind for the next meeting, an industry association visit.

Since arriving, you have been testing the Benny Lewis method to expand your linguistic skills. A polyglot author, Lewis tells his online tribe, Fluent in Three Months, that the most important part of speaking a new language is having "a direct motivation to live that language and use it as a means of communication and connection."[1] Motivations such as ordering meals, Lewis points out, push travelers into circumstances that are difficult but achievable and increase linguistic skill and confidence. He recommends that learners jump in and put themselves through as many

uncomfortable situations as possible. You know that not having a trans-
lator is a risk when going to the interview, but you sense it is a chance
worth taking.

The industry association representative, as it turns out, smiles at your
attempts to connect in his language. Your efforts prove sufficient, and
gesturing, a show-and-tell around the building, and conversations with
other staffers more familiar with your language are sufficient to close the
gap. Your visit is productive, and you leave full of notes and with a bigger
sense of the connections for your research.

One piece of information you don't have yet is survey data. This isn't
a major problem—your primary research goals involve on-the-ground
qualitative facts and analysis, not numbers and percentages—but surveys
can sometimes add a useful element for testing your research conclusions. One evening, sitting at your Airbnb desk after dinner, you consider
the circumstances when surveys are valuable and contemplate methods
for their conduct. After reviewing your interviews and field notes, you
decide survey data would be a useful addition.

You type out five questions that you would benefit from an unambig-
uous "yes" or "no" from the general public. You run the translations by
your friend, find a print shop, and make two hundred copies. You go to
bus stops, mall entrances, and busy street corners, offering the survey to
people of all ages and types. You smile, make eye contact, greet, and present one of the copies. About half wave you off immediately. But of the half
that stop to look, two-thirds accept the pen in your hand and complete the
survey form. It takes three days of steady effort, but eventually you have
197 responses.

———————

For field researchers, more data never hurts. I adopted the fictitious survey scenario above from real data a colleague and I collected on social
policy and cultural preferences for a client. The process we used—and
the research value of observing the respondents—was the same as what
I described. While this method of on-the-fly surveys is often taboo for
academic researchers because of compliance requirements for the Institutional Review Board, it can still be useful as a variable even if it is
inadmissible in published conclusions.

While the survey results were valuable in the client project I described
above, they essentially confirmed information and facts acquired from
interviews and observation. What was more valuable was each interac-

tion—seeing the various reactions to the survey across demographics and regions. Even though surveying in a public place is a short interaction, it allows for solid, useful data collection. It would not be wise to attempt a survey on your first day in the field. But by building confidence in meetings, interviews, and daily interactions, a field researcher can advance to a comfortable level for getting work done.

Although technical systems could have collected this information through online surveys or data mining, there is research value in taking a survey in person—yes, even when you can't speak the language. You can see how people react to your questions, your presence, and your earnest (if occasionally ineffective) efforts to bridge a cultural divide. These elements are qualitative data on their own, notwithstanding the information gained from the survey.

In field interactions that inherently involve short-term encounters, such as surveys or informal interviews, using an appropriate cover may be a helpful and necessary tool—especially when your research purposes and goals cannot be fully disclosed to the people whose information you seek. By "cover," I'm not suggesting anything fancy or foolish. Typically, there is very little need or value for you to pretend you are someone you are not when researching in another country. In the internet age, complete anonymity is a near impossibility. Cover, in this context, is a form of necessary behavior that leads to safer and more productive research interactions. Your intent is to be as honest as your research environment reasonably permits while also adhering to your company, college, or client's nondisclosure and/or ethical requirements. Your goal is to employ that elusive tactic called common sense.

For the field researcher, there are two prudent and practical methods of using cover. First, be selective about which facts you disclose to people you meet and the context in which you provide them. Let's say you are a freelance writer researching restaurants and have also gone to culinary school and worked on a kitchen staff. When talking to waiters or taxi drivers, you may decide to emphasize your restaurant background and skip the details about your research assignment—or perhaps the other way around. When you sense that drawing unnecessary attention to one aspect of your identity might make some people uncomfortable, go with the one they prefer and don't mention the one they wouldn't like. Truth, as they say, is the simplest ruse.

Second, observe whether or not the people you meet with are believing the rationale you've given for your presence and research purposes.

People everywhere are prone to think a "researcher" has a hidden agenda, and attempting to convince them otherwise often makes matters worse—both for you and them. Regardless of what you say and do, people will draw their own conclusions about who you are. Let them think whatever they want to think. It will make both of you more comfortable, whatever they decide your agenda is.

You check out of the Airbnb and spend your last night at a hotel, relaxing and preparing for your long trip ahead, just as you did on your first. You have a notebook full of observations, a stack of surveys, two dozen audio recordings from interviews and your own thoughts, and a file of digital photos. A few light souvenirs as well, but nothing you cannot carry in your own pack.

You make your way to the airport and process through customs and security. You board the plane, take your window seat, and smile as the aircraft ascends. You declined the free alcohol on the way in, but going back you have the wine with dinner. You are officially a field researcher. It's an accomplishment worth celebrating.

Key Points

· If you do not already know, learn how to say basic courtesies—thank you, please, hello, goodbye—in the local language as soon as possible upon arrival.

· At least once, take a taxi or hired driver who speaks your native language—such as when leaving the airport on your arrival. Paying extra fare is worth having a local contact.

· Team structure, task specifics, and expected length of stay are the most important variables that define a first day in the field.

· Whenever possible, field researchers should avoid making an interview their first field visit after arrival. Make initial contact on a friendly, collegial level. The purpose for the first meeting is for you to get comfortable talking to people in your new environment.

· Regardless of your level of foreign-language proficiency, use the Benny Lewis method while in the field: "The most important part of speaking a new language is . . . speaking a new language."

· Field surveys yield more than data. They also enable researchers to learn how people react to a researcher's questions and presence. These elements are qualitative data on their own.

- Using appropriate cover is a helpful and necessary tool, especially when your research goals cannot be fully disclosed to people whose information you seek.
- There are two prudent and practical methods to employ cover. First, be selective about which facts you disclose to people and the context you provide them. Second, observe whether or not people believe the rationale you offer for your presence and research.
- Trust your instincts and make decisions for your safety based on your own observations and judgments, which should be grounded in your situational awareness.

Note

1. Benny Lewis, *Fluent in 3 Months: How Anyone at Any Age Can Learn to Speak Any Language from Anywhere in the World* (New York: HarperCollins, 2014), 5.

6

The Interview

Interviewing is at the core of any field research project. Interviews come in all shapes and sizes, from a formal conversation in an office with questions in advance to a casual encounter in a mall jotted into a notebook. Along with experiential observations, interviews form the backbone of the two primary means of collecting data for any research project. Interviewing well in the field takes practice and patience.

In the previous chapter, we followed a new field researcher through several encounters on the ground and reflected on decisions made leading up to and following meetings and interviews. As we look at the interview itself, there are several aspects for consideration. Positionality and bias, as studied in earlier sections, play a role when collecting data from interviews. For example, the power dynamics—as positionality illustrates—differ substantially between a government researcher on a fact-finding mission and an academic researcher who must persuade an interviewee to remain a willing participant.[1]

A research interview is a delicate dance. And like any dance, there are strict rules to be broken, rigid forms to be altered, and disciplined structure from which to improvise. Interviewing is a microcosm of the entirety of field research: it's both an art and a science.

As noted, interviews come in all varieties. On one end of the spectrum is the casual coffee visit you later summarize in your field notebook. On the other might be a formal question-and-answer session recorded with a video production crew. Most field research interviewing is somewhere in the middle—usually a personal conversation recorded with a notebook or voice recorder. Researchers often prefer electronic audio files over video because audio files are often easier to manage with transcription software that can add the data into written documents.

In formal terms, researchers classify interviews in five different categories. *Structured interviews* involve questions created before the interview, with little variation or option for responses.[2] An interviewer is neutral, casual, and friendly—but usually not conversational. Self-administered questionnaires, such as the street survey described in the previous chapter, are also forms of structured interviews.[3] Developing one requires a clear topical focus, a well-developed set of questions, and guidelines the interviewer follows.

The most common field research interview is the *individual semi-structured interview*. The interviewer goes into a meeting with a list of questions and topics that need to be discussed in a conversation but also feels comfortable diverting from the established guidelines whenever it is appropriate.[4] Depending on the interview context and a researcher's relationship with the interviewee, semi-structured interviews may often require audio recordings instead of just written notes. A *focus group* is a group version of a semi-structured interview and, although less common in field research, follows a similar pattern and rhythm.[5]

An *unstructured interview* is a formal event where both parties meet for a conversation, but there is no specific agenda.[6] Researchers have a general understanding of the topic, focus, and goal of the conversation but guide the discussion without a definite direction. Unstructured interviews are particularly common in ethnographic work, where they are also labeled into subcategories of ethnographic unstructured interviews, which include oral history, creative interviews, and postmodern interviews.[7] As with semi-structured interviews, researchers often benefit from an audio recording of the interview, depending on whether or not rapport has been established for the interviewee to grant his or her consent.

Finally, an *informal interview* is the type of event we have often noted as a specific reason for field research: casual conversations in a setting that results from informal encounters where researchers are interviewing.[8] Informal interviews are just that—conversations that take place at random, unscheduled, unexpected intervals in the process of observing a setting. As we have learned, researchers then transcribe an informal interview into field notes from memory once the encounter is over.

Regardless of the country or circumstance, interviews have a typical protocol and follow a general pattern. Think of the way you have learned to write a research paper. As with an essay, interviews have an introduction, purpose, body, and conclusion. And like a good essay, the transitions between these parts should be smooth, natural, and fluid instead of sharp, harsh, or abrupt. A good interview should follow a natural rhythm, and a good field researcher senses the conversational flow and practices the art of adjusting accordingly. Let's consider the following scenario and examine how a typical field research interview might unfold.

———————

You have been sitting in the reception room for twenty minutes now and are starting to feel you have been waiting a long time. The delay is not entirely surprising, as it took several weeks for your visit to be approved. But time is cultural; it is part of the way people test you. The receptionist asks if you would like more tea.

Ten minutes later, your interviewee—a government official—opens the door, shaking your hand and offering profuse apologies for his tardiness. He ushers you into his office, seating you at a long oval conference table opposite him. A flag set decorates the table's center along with a tray of sweets and a candy dish. He motions to his secretary, and you accept yet another fresh cup of tea.

After you hand over your business card, the official asks where your colleagues are, noting that he thought he had been asked to "host a delegation." He appears somewhat put out that you are here alone. You apologize, saying your colleagues regret their absence, but there were multiple meetings and research efforts scheduled at the same time. Ordinarily you would have been here with a partner—hence the official's statements about the "delegation"—but multiple appointments meant you had to split up.

You register the comment as an implicit transition from introductions and move on to discussing the purpose of your visit. You are here to evaluate the results of a border management program designed to benefit infrastructure, migration, and trade. While the official is inclined to be helpful, he also feels it is necessary to demonstrate to researchers like you that the "capacity building investment" has been positive. From conversations with his staff prior to the meeting, you sense he is somewhat concerned that if he is not courteous, the resources that international organizations have been offering for the program might go away. There is an uncertain power dynamic in your conversation as you sit down to begin, and he is looking at you, anticipating your first question.

———————

The scientific aspects of interviewing are relatively straightforward. Mirror your interviewee's expected clothing. If you are going to an office, wear business attire. Have a notebook pad with pen and a voice recorder, if permitted (and always check first). Arrive on time to show respect, even if you are told the culture is tolerant of tardiness. Make sure your questions are clear when asked. Avoid loaded or accusatory lines of questioning as well as questions easily answered with only a yes or no. Persuade interviewees to open up, and give them time to complete their thoughts during your conversation.

The art of interviewing lies in the decisions an interviewer makes within the context of implementing the science described above. For example, mirroring an interviewee's clothing and style are often snap choices made immediately in the moment. Do you remove your jacket and hang it on the back of your chair because your interviewee has an open collar and sleeves rolled up? Then, what cues will tell you when it is time to move beyond casual banter and into the substance of your interview visit? Finally, how can you discuss sensitive subjects and obtain the information you need without offending your interlocutor?

The introduction phase of interviews involves welcoming, seating, and offering a beverage—varying for each culture, but usually coffee, tea, or water. Pick something when asked—letting your host serve you is not only good manners but also part of breaking down defensiveness and gaining trust. If your interviewee is your senior, he or she will likely move to title introductions and business card exchanges. You will be expected to do the same if you are senior to your interlocutor. If you are peers, casual pleasantries about your experience in a new country may continue on for some time before you exchange business cards.

Yes, it is important to have real business cards available for these types of occasions. If you are a freelancer, print some out that look sharp. Even though most contact information is electronic, the tangibility of business cards is still preferred worldwide in an introduction, and it would usually be seen as impolite to move forward without having performed this professional ritual. In many cultures, business cards are offered and accepted with two hands in meetings; use this technique if in doubt. There is rarely harm in showing extra respect.

After beverages, pleasantries, and business cards are finished, you will be expected to talk briefly about the purpose of your visit and what you hope to learn or accomplish. If you are an academic researcher, this is the appropriate time to handle your Institutional Review Board requirements for research (such as ethical disclosures, privacy statements, and, if necessary, release forms or waivers). For a corporate researcher or freelancer, you will need to assess the conversation and decide how much candor is required to maintain an interviewee's trust while adhering to your nondisclosure agreement. For a government researcher, this is the time to say what the stated "official" reason is for your visit—to discuss the program you represent and briefly describe the type of facts you have traveled thousands of miles to find.

The most important part of this phase is not so much what you say but observing and evaluating an interviewee's reaction to the purpose you disclose. When you are first speaking, you may notice your interviewee's body language become thoughtful, perhaps even tense. They are consciously and subconsciously considering your purpose and deciding how much of their own information they will feel comfortable sharing over the course of your conversation.

Your goal is to move through this phase as smoothly and quickly as possible; there is no value in belaboring or repeating your purpose statement any longer than necessary. Every interviewee will signal confidence and acceptance of your proposed interview purpose differently. A challenge for a field researcher may come if the interviewee appears to reject your objective for the interview and informs you, both in what they say and do not say, that they have a different agenda for accepting the meeting than you did.

This leads us back to power dynamics. In any discourse, power—defined as controlling and constraining the dialogue—is constantly negotiated between participants.[9] Interviewers, for example, exercise power by setting an agenda and asking certain questions.[10] Interviewees can assert power by deciding which questions they want to answer or which portions of an interview agenda they wish to accept.[11]

Assessments, calculations, and adjustments associated with power dynamics between an interviewer and interviewee are present from the beginning of the encounter. For government researchers conducting program assessments or fact-finding missions, their very presence represents an extension of their government's power, and the entire conversation will be an analogue of the power relationship between the two countries represented. An interview like this is almost always dominated by the government researcher, with an interviewee retaining power only by revealing or withholding information.

In academic research, power is often more fluid. If an interviewee is reluctant to provide information, alters the flow of conversation, or begins posing their own questions, there is little an interviewer can do to hurry or compel their conversant.[12] The experienced interviewer, recognizing this power shift, can move to balance the power dynamic by courting an interviewee—by enhancing the sense of rapport, building a sympathetic relationship, and developing a mutual trust in completing the research interview.[13] A good interviewer strives to create a fluid power balance: encouraging an interviewee to explore broad topics while still retaining control of the conversational flow so the research goals are achieved.

You both already know why you are there, but courtesy requires talking it through anyway. The official is polite as you opaquely mention your interest in discussing border security improvements, and you are careful not to ask a direct question in order to evaluate his reaction and see what he says. You had an interest in conducting a site visit but are not yet sure if you should bring it up in conversation or if he will do so. In response to your comment, he brings up both the funding organization and your research sponsor, telling you how pleased he has been to have "opportunities for mutual collaboration." This verbal dance goes on for several minutes, although it feels like it takes much longer than it actually does.

Unprompted, the official launches into a detailed explanation of the tactics and techniques the border guards have been training in in recent months. You open your notebook, moving into the meeting's substance a bit sooner than expected. As with the introductions, the interviewee has been controlling the pace; you did not get to ask the first question, which will leave you less time to investigate the topics you want to discuss. You make a mental note of the power dynamic.

While you are taking notes, the official reaches over to his desk, shuffles through a stack of files, and hands you a thick folder with tabs and labels. You have two thoughts. First, this is a gold mine of information, containing practically everything you have traveled to learn about for your research. Second, and more importantly, the official has revealed his own agenda by pre-packaging all of the information he knows would portray the border program in the most positive light. You feel as though he is telling you what he thinks you want to hear, which causes you to instinctively question the information's authenticity.

The official continues speaking. Outwardly, you are listening, nodding, and writing. In your mind, you are weighing your options and considering your next move. He turns over the last page, hands you the entire document, and asks if you need anything else. It is clear he would like for the meeting to be over. You, on the other hand, have not yet asked a single independent question. He may be finished, but in terms of your own goals for the research interview, you are barely getting started.

The transition from discussing the purpose of an interview into a meeting's actual substance varies with each encounter. Over coffee or drinks, elements of an unstructured interview might occur during the entire casual conversation, which you simply file away and record later in your notebook. In an office, an interviewee may simply state a desire to get started and not say anything else until you pull out your voice recorder and begin questioning.

Two things are important about the transition into the main body of your interview. First, you must be consciously aware that it has happened. If you intend to use a voice recorder, it should be turned on; if you are taking notes, your notebook should be out. Second, you must evaluate the power dynamic associated with how the transition took place. Have you been invited to control the conversational tempo, or does your interviewee have his or her own agenda? The manner in which the interview starts will set a tone for the rest of the dialogue.

If you are interviewing with a partner or as part of a research team, you should go into a meeting with a general plan of who will do what during the interview. Interview partners can make or break each other, depending on their own levels of experience and awareness. Ideally, you should decide beforehand if you will share equal time with your partner or if one will take the lead in questioning and the other will be observing, taking notes, and only chiming in if necessary to follow up.

That said, things don't always work according to plan, and your partner may have developed an unanticipated rapport with an interviewee in ways that neither of you had previously anticipated. Be comfortable with your partner's style. If possible, practice interviewing together with another colleague role-playing an interview, and then conduct after-actions and discuss observations. Above all else, never contradict your partner or teammate during an interview. Disagreements and differences of opinion should be discussed and resolved in private and are never appropriate in front of an interviewee.

As each conversational topic unfolds, you should observe your interviewee's body language. If a line of questioning appears to disturb an interviewee, consider steering the conversation away from the sensitive topic and onto something more casual. If you are in his or her office, observe the pictures, plaques, and other iconography and, if appropriate, comment on any similarities you might share in experiences or interests.

If your interviewee has taken control of the meeting, keep recording the information you are receiving while paying close attention to what they are not telling you as well. In many cases, there is no malicious or negative intent by the interviewee if they are controlling the tempo. They may have a busy day and just want to get you out of their office. Or they may think they already know what you need to know better than you do.

At the same time, your goal as a researcher is to be thorough and detailed with your questions and not just accept the documents, statements, and other information you are receiving at face value. Ask follow-up or clarifying questions when there are pauses in conversation. If you are not allowed to speak for most of the meeting, make notes on the questions that have not been answered.

If you have backed off from sensitive topics, engaged with lighthearted banter, and still feel the interview going into a tailspin, your last resort is to approach the problem directly. Tell your interviewee that you sense they are uncomfortable and ask if there is anything else they would like to discuss. This is too confrontational an approach for most situations, particularly if you and your interviewee have just met. But if you are already acquainted with each other, have been interviewed before, or simply feel that candor will be effective, a direct question may be more appropriate to determine where things went off track.

As with all things in field research, you must ultimately learn your own interview style through trial and error, just as you develop your own research style. Interviewing in the field is interwoven with the research process, and collecting data successfully is as much an expression of who you are as the penmanship in your notebook. Some techniques will work better for you than for other researchers, and some will not. Test different approaches and note what is more effective for you and why.

Not every interview can be as productive as you want, but time in conversation is never wasted. Stall tactics, smoke screens, and general rudeness are all, in and of themselves, forms of qualitative data. Simply note the interview content you did receive, record relevant observations, and keep moving forward with your research. As with many things in life, patience and perseverance often eventually pay off in interviews.

Although the official seems to want the visit to be over, you still need to ask a few questions. But questioning at this moment does not seem like it would be effective; you need to rebalance the power dynamic—and fast— or you will lose the opportunity to get the necessary information. You decide it is time to find something else to discuss.

At the beginning of the interview, when you had first walked into the room, you happened to notice a framed, autographed picture of the French 2006 World Cup team on the official's wall. You mention the photo and comment admiringly, noting the team's misfortune in the final match against Italy. As he smiles and relaxes, you both relive the highs and lows of the 2006 World Cup final for ten minutes, recalling each goal, offside, and penalty kick from memory. By the time you finish, you have both concluded France would have found a way to win if only their star player, Zinedine Zidane, had remained on the pitch.

The conversational diversion has relaxed the official, and now you have your opening. You ask if you can speak with any graduates of the border training courses. He sighs. "There have been a few delays in program implementation," he says, finally relenting and spending the next ten minutes telling you most of what you need to know. The document he gave you is still useful because now you know everything that was supposed to happen.

But the interview has told you what is actually happening. As you suspected, the program funding appears to have mostly been spent on developing training curriculum rather than on implementation. The official spends a few minutes explaining the delays, telling you the problem will be smoothed over with next year's funding. Things will go even faster, he says with a smile, if the research report you are preparing demonstrates the training curriculum's value. You smile, nod, and tell him you will note his comments.

You finish writing and close your notebook, satisfied that you have found at least some of the facts you have traveled to research. One of your purposes in coming here was to persuade officials to open up with information that you have not been able to confirm with your existing data. Combined with the document—most of which you already have on file— the official's comments should prove sufficient for your report.

But additional data sources never hurt, which is why you have learned that the most important question to ask in the interview is always last.

"Do you know anyone else I should talk to while I am here?" you ask the official.[14] He smiles, nods, and calls to his assistant.

Finishing the interview in this way does two things. First, more often than not, an interviewee does know someone else—and will provide that person's contact information only after finishing the interview, not at the beginning. Second, if the interview has gone well, you are able to affirm the connection by asking for and receiving a favor from your interviewee in the form of a new contact. This retains a positive rapport, sustains a power balance, and affirms mutual trust between both interviewer and interviewee when concluding the in-person meeting.

The official escorts you back into the lobby. "Come and see me next time you are in town," he says cheerfully. And he tells you to say hi to his friend—a foreign ministry official whose phone number and email the assistant provided.

You walk out of the building. A driver is waiting to take you back to the hotel where you will meet another member of your research team. You sit and review your notes. The interview turned out even better than you had expected.

Key Points

- Interviewing is a microcosm of field research: it's both an art and a science.
- The five types of research interviews are structured, individual semi-structured, focus group, unstructured, and informal interview.
- Interviews have a typical protocol and follow a general pattern of an introduction, purpose, body, and conclusion.
- The introduction phase of official interviews usually involves welcoming, seating, offering a beverage—usually coffee, tea, or water—and exchanging business cards.
- It is important to have real business cards available for interviews. In many cultures, business cards are offered and accepted with two hands in meetings.
- When discussing the purpose of your interview, observe and evaluate your interviewee's reaction to the purpose you disclose, and take note of the power dynamic present as you do so. Do not skip this phase, but move through it as quickly as possible.
- A good interviewer strives to create a fluid power balance: encouraging an interviewee to explore broad topics while still re-

taining control of the conversational flow so the research goals are achieved.

- If an interviewee has taken control of the meeting, record the information being received, pay attention to what they are not disclosing, and look for opportunities to rebalance the power dynamic.
- If you are interviewing with a partner or team, be comfortable with and play off of your co-interviewer's style. Never contradict your partner or teammate in front of an interviewee.
- When concluding the interview, always ask an interviewee if he or she knows anyone else you should talk to. This generally ends the interview on a positive note.

Notes

1. Frederick Anyan, "The Influence of Power Shifts in Data Collection and Analysis Stages: A Focus on Qualitative Research Interview," *The Qualitative Report* 18 (2013): 1–9.
2. D. Cohen and B. Crabtree, "Qualitative Research Guidelines Project," July 2006, http://www.qualres.org/HomeSemi-3629.html.
3. Ibid.
4. Ibid.
5. Ibid.
6. Ibid.
7. Ibid.
8. Ibid.
9. Anyan, "The Influence of Power Shifts," 2.
10. Ibid.
11. Ibid.
12. Ibid., 5.
13. Ibid.
14. The reporter David Halberstam was best known for this maxim.

The Field
Review Questions

Chapter 4: Logistics and Networking
- On what basis should field research itineraries be developed? Will they look the same or different from tourist schedules?
- What are the three largest international airline partner networks? Why are they important to know when booking airline travel?
- How should you approach airline ticket purchasing online? What types of techniques can be used to develop a cheaper itinerary?
- On what two occasions should a field researcher plan to stay in a nice hotel? What are examples of other types of lodging that will be more beneficial for field research?
- Are lodging plans usually different if a field researcher is traveling often while in the field instead of staying in a single location? Why or why not?
- What is the name of the booklet medical professionals should transcribe your vaccinations into before you go overseas?
- How should a researcher carry cash and credit cards while in the field?
- What variables should a field researcher consider when building up an initial network?

Chapter 5: On the Ground
- Why is it useful to take a taxi or hired driver who speaks English soon after arriving? How does this benefit a field researcher?
- What are the variables that typically define a field researcher's first day? How are these different for research teams instead of solo field researchers?
- What is the purpose of the first meeting in the field? What type of contact is best to meet with for the first field visit after arrival?

- What is the Benny Lewis method of language learning? Why is it important to use while in the field?
- What types of qualitative data can field research surveys yield that are different and separate from the quantitative data collected? Why is this important?
- Why is it sometimes necessary in fieldwork to use appropriate cover?
- What are two prudent and practical methods of employing cover?
- If you are planning to go into the field, how would you handle the scenario described in the chapter? What techniques would you apply differently? Why?

Chapter 6: The Interview

- In what way is interviewing a microcosm of field research?
- What are the five types of research interviews?
- What does the introduction phase of official interviews usually involve? Are business cards important to have available? If so, why?
- What is the power dynamic between interviewers and interviewees? Why is it important?
- What two things are important about the transition from discussing the purpose of your interview to the main body of the meeting?
- What defines a healthy interview power balance? How should you proceed when you are in control of the interview flow? How should you respond if your interviewee takes control of the meeting?
- How will you prepare differently for an interview if you are working with a partner or team? What should you never do in this circumstance?
- What question should you always ask an interviewee when concluding the interview?
- What choices in the interview scenario did this field researcher make that you agreed with? What did you disagree with? Why?

PART III
Finishing Touches

7

Objectivity Is a Myth

When I was about six, I discovered a weathered geography textbook that, decades earlier, had belonged to my mother. The flags of every country in the world were listed alphabetically inside the front and back covers. For fun, I drew the flags with crayons and colored pencils, then challenged myself to match as many as possible to the interior maps inside the textbook. The world's banners fascinated me. I was amazed at how shapes and symbols and fabric and color could inspire such vast differences in identity throughout the world. I still am today.

Somewhere around the time I was matching those horribly sketched flags to actual places, I found myself aspiring to experience every single one of them. I did not know then, but I wanted to understand the thrill Russians felt when swimming in Lake Baikal after enduring their frigid Siberian winter, or the communal harmony of the *hamam*, or Turkish bath, used for centuries for weekly cleaning and relaxation. I did not want to learn about these things just from reading about them. I wanted to experience them with all five senses and physically know what they were like.

I still feel this same desire to understand every country in the world, even though I sense I am unlikely to do so in my lifetime. Even with modernity's air transportation system, those who attempt the audacious feat of visiting every country might travel to places without having really seen or understood them when their journey is over. Can I claim to know Algeria if I have been to Algiers but not to the Atlas Mountains or in the southern deserts of Tamanrasset? Do I understand Turkmenistan if I have never explored anything beyond a hectic itinerary in the capital city of Ashgabat? Will I leave Macedonia with a sense of what makes it different from Greece if I have never ventured beyond the banks of the Vardar River in Skopje?

Although I have completed field research in the countries and cities I just mentioned, I eventually left each place with a deeper sense of what I had not seen. Traveling there, while enlightening, also provided me with a more profound awareness of the borders I had not yet crossed. In each case, knowing the limitations of what I had researched proved essential both for delivering the client's final product and for reflecting on, and maintaining, my own humanity during the process.

For example, by not going to the Atlas Mountains or Algeria's deserts, I could not genuinely describe the sense of grievance or rural alienation farmers and nomads might feel toward Algiers. Not seeing Turkmenistan's tribal villages living the daily rhythms of ancient religions meant I could not sense their conflict with the urban atheism dominating Ashgabat. Not traveling to the ethnic Albanian region near Macedonia's border meant I could not fully grasp the ethnic divisions that had fueled conflict—and how powerful it was for Macedonia's national story that, in 1999, the two factions, through dialogue, halted several episodes of violence.

Before and After

Destin Sandlin, an American engineer from Alabama, thought he knew how to ride a bicycle—until he tried to do it in a completely different way. One day, a colleague rigged a bike so the front wheel turned right when pointing the handlebars left, and vice versa. Dared to ride this "backwards bicycle," Sandlin thought he could do so in a few minutes. Instead, it took him eight months, practicing five minutes a day, before he could retrain his brain to master the skill.[1]

Sandlin's story serves as an object lesson in the effects of cognitive bias. Once his brain had learned to ride the backward bike, Sandlin was unable to ride a regular bicycle. It took twenty minutes of practice before Sandlin's brain regained the ability to ride a normal bike. His parting thoughts after the experiment? "Be very careful how you interpret things, because you're looking at the world with a bias whether you think you are or not."

Before you went into the field, you probably thought you had a good sense of why you were going. And when you were there, some of what you experienced was what you had expected. But other parts of the journey surprised you with what they made you feel. You had gone in with a thesis, and some of the information you have collected now challenges your theory even as other data support it.

Throughout the time you have been assimilating your observations, you noticed yourself and your opinions and perspectives—we might even say, your positionality—changing while you were in the field. When you would FaceTime or Skype with your loved ones, you struggled to explain the things you were thinking and feeling. Observations and conversations left a deeper mental and emotional imprint on your professional and personal psyche than you thought they would. And the evolution makes you feel less and less certain of how to evaluate factual accuracy. At this point, you aren't even sure what objectivity looks like.

This chapter discusses the struggle field researchers face when striving for objectivity in using the data they have collected *after* they have been to the field. If you leave your research destination with a strong contrast from your original expectations, the resulting duality invariably impacts the way you will evaluate data and consider conclusions. If you have felt kindness where you expected cruelty, witnessed brutality when you anticipated compassion, or seen weakness where you expected strength, the bias you feel has become different from what it was before you left.

If you fell in love with the place you traveled to, it might make you blind to flaws that other researchers have observed. If your trip was miserable, you might be repulsed by people who describe the region you visited in positive terms. Whatever the case, your experience is tainted in certain ways because you have seen both worlds but know only parts of each. You may have assumed traveling would make it easier to identify your predispositions and understand the Other, but that hasn't turned out to be as true as you had hoped it would be. On the contrary, you are now *more* subjective, only in new and different ways.

Your New Minority Status

As an experienced field researcher, you have now become a minority, with biases that have, as all biases are, been shifted and shaped by your experiences. Your minority status is not ethnic or cultural but informational and experiential. "If you're a minority, you are always aware that your experiences, view and perspective are different," writes Lane Wallace. "You can't possibly mistake any of that for some kind of accepted norm or pure, objective truth."[2]

Wallace, a female pilot and adventure writer, is a minority in her own profession—94 percent of the aviation field's employees are male. She says her experience as a female pilot—as part of the 6 percent—has taught her more about how norms, assumptions, and biases shape responses than anything else in her life. "Experiences give us a particular set of lenses through which we view the world," she writes. "They influence how much weight we give to different factors in an argument, and what we tend to believe out of what we're told."[3]

Field researching brings a rare form of expertise to those who learn the science and practice the art. Because the capability is uncommon within an organization or industry—after all, not everyone can go out for field research—the minority status it brings can be jarring. You may not have expected your colleagues to be envious or jealous of your new perspectives or fresh insights, but they are. And that emotion—itself a response lacking in objectivity—may fuel stronger criticism of your work than you expect.

Know What Is Missing

Before you start building out the story of your fieldwork—a process addressed in the next chapter—there is an important series of questions to ask and answer about your research material. How can you most accurately describe what you witnessed? What are the limits of your observations? How much confidence do you have in the data you received from your sources? What type of information are you missing? Are you able to describe what you did not observe, and why? Can you narrate as clearly what you did not see as well as what you did?

There are two deeper motives for asking these questions. First, by looking for the gaps in your data, you are certain to find something that is absent. Acknowledging these weaknesses up front strengthens the quality and credibility of what you do have. Second, identifying omissions reinforces a healthy unpretentiousness about your work. Amateur field researchers boast about having "been there." Professionals come back more mystified than when they left. This attitude impacts the way a field researcher of any type—academic, government, or corporate—examines and presents their data, reports, and conclusions.

In previous chapters, we have looked at how people rely on nonverbal senses to subconsciously gather and process information about each other. As we have learned, our perception capabilities about a place extend beyond our five senses and into the "feel" we have of its intangibles. This is among the many reasons why it is so important to take notes on your observations, thoughts, and feelings while in the field. The only reasonable way you can make sense of what you feel about your data—particularly when others who have shared your experience reach different conclusions—is by looking back at your own reflections.

As the poet Wallace Stevens writes,

Twenty men crossing a bridge,
Into a village,
Are twenty men crossing twenty bridges,
Into twenty villages,
Or one man
Crossing a single bridge into a village.[4]

Freelance journalism offers a useful illustration of how research professionals grapple with this reality. "The oft-stated and highly desired goal of modern journalism is objectivity, the detached and unprejudiced gathering and dissemination of news and information," writes Richard Taflinger, an associate professor of communications at Washington State University. "It's a pity that such a goal is impossible to achieve."[5] How do journalists decide what is "objective reporting" while also knowing the best they can do is describe what they have perceived?

"If reporters are aware that their world view is a component of the news, then reporters . . . will consciously minimize the impact of subjectivity," writes Taflinger. "They will examine their work to be sure that prejudice, bias, and a personal world view is not the one that dominates."[6] The same is true for field researchers evaluating and presenting their work, much like positionality affects a personal research style.

There is a certain irony to this. As we have discussed, one of the primary reasons for going into the field often involves overcoming your inherent biases. Awareness of your natural prejudices was supposed to enable you to expand your horizons, not make you more predisposed to a certain way of thinking. But now, you inevitably have new biases, and it becomes even more important to understand and admit them as you evaluate your data.

Old Bias versus New Bias

When you first start preparing for field research, it is comparatively easy to acknowledge the environmental influences that have shaped you. After finishing your research project, however, you are still biased—but now in ways that fewer people can understand. Whether you like it or not, your life as a fieldworker makes you a member of a rare tribe. Those who are paid to travel and write usually need not say anything more than where they last went to satisfy those who have sought their perspective.

As a research professional, of course you want to be objective. You should be. Objectivity, however, is somewhat like perfection—noble to strive for, yet impossible to attain. As you read your notes and frame your data, keep in mind that you are now part of a new narrative—one that is, in a different way, as limiting as not having been there. Whether you were in the field for two weeks or two years, you saw some things, but not everything. You know more questions to ask than before about the areas where you were researching but still lack knowledge of at least some of the relevant cultural nuances. Your objectivity is still tainted, only differently than before.

Narrating your experience and sharing your conclusions is, thus, a less objective process than you may want it to be. Describing what happened in your interviews or building a matrix from your field notes and surveys will likely result in qualitative and/or quantitative data. But that data, objective as it is, still has a bias, an origin, a source. Paradoxically, it can often become more difficult to identify the type and origin of your biases after you have been in the field. You want your data and facts to speak for themselves because you collected them, because you were there. For many field researchers, this is the point where they need to be careful, lest their ego obscure progress on their research path.

Letting Go of Ego

Organizational environments are competitive. As a field researcher, it's important to remember that colleagues and rivals who haven't had field experience—or who have done different kinds of research—may feel threatened by your new knowledge. As you assess your material, you should remain conscious that some may attack your observations simply in an effort to bolster their own status. When placed under stress, humans naturally respond by running away or attacking. Sometimes, a field researcher responds to a coworker or colleague's attack by pushing data forward that, while incomplete, assuages their own sense of self.

There may not be anything fundamentally wrong with this—experience is certainly a valid rhetorical defense—but it may also be an inadequate response. Is there a healthier, more useful way for the field researcher to handle organizational competition while also pursuing the objectivity

ideal? Is it possible to accept that objectivity is a myth in a way that goes
on to enhance the strength of a field researcher's final product?

Yes. Not only is it possible, it is necessary. For if you intend to assemble the report, prepare the presentation, or confirm the recommendations, your work is made stronger, not weaker, by identifying up front the
limitations within the material your field research informs. This sounds
easy but is challenging to accomplish. After all, you have been there. You
have seen and felt and tasted and smelled and sensed and lived in this
other place while your colleagues were taking it easy, back in the office.
Why shouldn't they listen to you? Why can't they understand?

Effectively managing the data, notes, and information you've collected
so you can use that data to tell an effective story requires a series of mental
tricks that take on the quality of Zen riddles. Look at the information and
let what is there speak for itself. What do your notes say? What don't they
say? If you find yourself analyzing your data with an eye toward needing
to prove something to someone else, take a moment, pause, breathe, and
let it go. To effectively employ your material, you must consciously avoid
seeking to accomplish anything with it.

Understanding your limitations does not delegitimize your research
but, on the contrary, will enhance your capacity to communicate what you
did see. By identifying what you have missed, you will thwart unnecessary
and unhelpful criticism from those who would compete with you against
your will. Admitting awareness of your biases also increases the chances
that jealous and fearful colleagues will disclose the limitations of their
own objectivity. This reduces the competitive aspect that often emerges
in post–field research organizational evaluations, which enables everyone concerned to make better use of your data.

Above all, field research should inspire a deep sense of wonder within
those of us fortunate enough to practice it as a profession. As Walter Mc-
Dougall, a University of Pennsylvania history professor, wrote about his
own scholastic subject, "Students [of history] will acquire a sense of the
contingency of all human endeavor, the gaping disparity between motives
and consequences in all human action, and how little control human be-
ings have over their own lives and those of others."[7] Although McDougall
was discussing how research impacted history students, he could have
just as easily been referencing how time in other places affects field researchers.

As returning explorers, constraining our observations with a healthy
dose of humility regarding the things we did not learn and see while in the

field gives us greater confidence when communicating what we did learn and see. By identifying the changes to our positionality, we can at least increase our level of objectivity within the limits of that particular lens. Striving for objectivity in reporting our data, observations, and conclusions should inspire a sense of awe, reverence, and respect for the scope of how much we do not know.

A few years ago, I hung a laminated upside-down world map in my office. At first, my colleagues laughed, thinking it was a gimmick. My intention was different: I wanted to challenge myself to look at the world each day in a new way—to examine the map from a perspective that is just as accurate but opposite from the "objective" reality I had understood as exclusive since I was drawing those flags at age six. I knew from traveling that my own view of the world, even when looking at a map, was shaped by my own subjective cartographic perception.

As I later learned, turning the world upside down may have helped me see more than just the world differently. Arjun Appadurai, University of Chicago anthropology professor, explains how inverting objectivity deepens a researcher's imagination in his critique of Western area studies. "We need to ask ourselves what it means to internationalize any sort of research before we can apply our understandings to the [mapped] geography of areas and regions," writes Appadurai. "In essence, this requires a closer look at research as a practice of the imagination."[8]

When we studied the fictitious scenarios of researchers on the ground for their first few days or evaluated the interview with the government official, we did not dismiss any of the imagined observations or conclude they were flawed in collecting data; we looked at what they found relative to how we pictured their perception as we mentally envisioned the scenario. Field research material is just that: the imagined substance of what a researcher learns and sees. But by knowing what we have not seen, we also gain imaginative energy to glimpse new design possibilities. The restrictions we place on ourselves by knowing what we did not observe fuel greater creative potential, not the other way around.

A clear and healthy awareness of your material's limitations will enable you to sort through what is most useful as you prepare to build your material into the story for your colleagues and clients. And as you do so, shedding the myth of objectivity releases you of the unhelpful burden of measuring your accomplishments with envious others. As a confident professional, you know there is only one person you ever need to compete with: yourself.

Key Points

- Field researching brings a rare form of expertise to those who learn the science and practice the art. Because the expertise that field research brings is itself uncommon within an organization or industry, the minority status that goes along with it can be jarring.
- Before you start building out the story of your fieldwork, ask and answer a series of questions about what is and is not contained in your research material.
- When you first start preparing for field research, it is comparatively easy to acknowledge the environmental influences that have shaped your reactions. After finishing your research, you are still biased—but now in ways that few can understand.
- Look for the gaps in your data. You are certain to find some. Acknowledging these weaknesses up front strengthens the quality and credibility of the material you have. By identifying what you have missed, you will thwart unnecessary and unhelpful criticism.
- Above all else, the opportunity to practice the art and science of field research should inspire a deep sense of humility within those fortunate enough to call it their profession.

Notes

1. Ayun Halliday, "Discover The Backwards Brain Bicycle: What Riding a Bike Says about the Neuroplasticity of the Brain," Open Culture, August 21, 2015, accessed January 24, 2016, http://www.openculture.com/2015/08/the-backwards-brain -bicycle.html.
2. Lane Wallace, "The Myth of Objectivity," *The Atlantic*, July 14, 2009, http://www .theatlantic.com/national/archive/2009/07/the-myth-of-objectivity/21217/.
3. Ibid.
4. Wallace Stevens, "Metaphors of a Magnifico," in *The Collected Poems of Wallace Stevens* (New York: Knopf, 1954), 17. The poem was originally published in 1918.
5. Richard F. Taflinger, "The Myth of Objectivity in Journalism: A Commentary," Washington State University, ERMCC, May 29, 1996, http://public.wsu.edu/~ta-flinge/mythobj.html.
6. Ibid.
7. Walter A. McDougall, "The Three Reasons We Teach History," Foreign Policy Research Institute, February 1, 1998, http://www.fpri.org/article/1998/02/the -three-reasons-we-teach-history/.
8. Arjun Appadurai, "Grassroots Globalization and the Research Imagination," *Public Culture* 12, no. 1 (Winter 2000): 1–19.

8

Telling the Story

The fictional scenario in this chapter asks you to consider yourself an academic field researcher on a short deadline to present data.

You have been back from Lahore for almost ten days now. Pakistan's daily rhythms have faded from memory; you no longer hear the dozens, perhaps hundreds, of *muezzin* calling the faithful to prayer five times daily. Your sleep cycle has just reset to your home time zone, and your body has acclimated back to cooler weather after three months of sultry humidity.

The academic fellowship was a success. Your colleagues from the University of Lahore welcomed your collaboration to their philology curriculum and biweekly guest lectures for their American studies graduate students. And better yet, you were able to explore most of the country. You met with colleagues, acquaintances, and friends from Peshawar, Islamabad, Karachi, Quetta, and even the Balochi city of Turbat. The observations, information, and data you collected from these visits filled four notebooks—two of which were purchased from Lahore supermarkets. The breadth and scope of your experience surpassed even your highest expectations.

Now comes the hard part. At least it feels more difficult than perhaps it should, since an evening lecture for students and department faculty should not seem like a daunting assignment for an assistant professor. Still, you can't help but feel overwhelmed by the scope of what the audience expects during a twenty-minute talk followed by a question-and-answer conversation. How do you present so much material in such a short time accurately, effectively, and clearly?

How do you tell the story?

Everything Is Story

Before narrating your field experience in a presentation, report, article, podcast, documentary, or any other form, the first thing you must remember is that you are, in fact, telling a story. By this, I do not mean that you are making up events or fictionalizing your material. Assembling and arranging the data and information you collected requires choosing some elements of your material over others. If done properly, whatever sequence you select informs, enlightens, and entertains those who are reading, watching, or listening. A story is nothing more—and nothing less.

Fair enough. But informing, enlightening, and entertaining is a tall order for anyone to accomplish when competing against modern communication. Holding the attention span of today's observer, listener, or reader long enough to avert their eyes from checking email, scanning headlines, or texting friends on a tablet or smartphone is an accomplishment in and of itself. Doing this requires one thing: telling a compelling story.

Story Elements

Rather than attempt to explain the full structure and form of story—which could take an entire book—let's start with the basic elements. Over two thousand years ago, the philosopher Aristotle became the first person in what we've come to call the Western world known to have outlined the core components of a story. In his work *On Rhetoric*, the Greek scholar defined *ethos*, *pathos*, and *logos* as the elements that must exist somewhere in any presentation—spoken or written—for the material, and speaker, to connect with an audience. *Ethos* means credibility: does the tone, substance, and content of your material establish your authority with listeners on the topic? *Pathos* describes the emotions you evoke: will your readers feel compassion, frustration, sympathy, fear, and/or love as they experience your time in the field? *Logos* is factual accuracy: will your observers see and comprehend the rationale behind your perspective as you tell them about your experience?[1]

If ethos, pathos, and logos are the elements required in a story, then how do field researchers identify which data, interviews, and observations they can categorize and classify to bring out these elements? The initial step might surprise you. Do not start building the story without first knowing which nonfiction genre best suits the information you have collected. Once you know what genre you are working in, you can start sorting out which facts will best fuse ethos, pathos, and logos together for your audience.

The Four Nonfiction Genres

As we sort our material into story elements, we identify which items will establish credibility (ethos), call forth emotion (pathos), or rationally prove our thesis (logos). But labeling the data we have collected will not be enough on its own to create a story. Taking the next step in getting your research on paper or into a presentation requires knowing the different categories, or genres, into which nonfiction work can be organized.

Shawn Coyne, a longtime writer, editor, and publisher who blogs at www.storygrid.com, sorts nonfiction into four main genres: Academic, How-To, Narrative Nonfiction, and The Big Idea. On his blog, Coyne analyzes each of these nonfiction genres, in addition to five major fiction genres, through an editorial tool he developed called The Story Grid. When Coyne has a manuscript to edit, he filters it through this "grid," which drives his wordsmithing choices.

Academic genre material, Coyne says, is written and presented for a focused audience of specialists.[2] This group is clearly defined, small in number, and deeply dedicated to the nuances of specific passions or professions. A field researcher working in the Academic style will typically be more attentive to presenting findings logically than keeping readers or listeners entertained. This is because the audience already understands the nuances of the material (as examples from technical academic presentations often illustrate) and wants to know specific pieces of information that enhance their expertise.

The How-To genre denotes work presented as a tool for an audience's trade.[3] What is the best way to drive new business, plant a garden, or design a city? For the field researcher, a How-To audience will be more general than an Academic group and will be interested in a basic level of knowledge or a solution on something they can do to improve their lives. Examples of this range from martial arts techniques to health lifestyle choices to food and coffee recipes originally cultivated in one culture and then imported to another.

Narrative Nonfiction genre content, particularly in writing, uses techniques common in fiction to explain why an event happened instead of simply stating it as fact.[4] This form weaves a theme and controlling idea through a narrative so the writer (or presenter) is not only stating what happened but making a subjective case or interpretation of the truth behind it. The classic American example of this category is Truman Capote's *In Cold Blood*, the true (and field researched) story of four murders in Kansas and the subsequent conviction and execution of the killers. The concepts behind Narrative Nonfiction have so permeated the language of modern media that politicians, journalists, and public relations staff spend most of their days discussing and debating their "narrative." In presentation terms, Narrative Nonfiction is what PowerPoint was supposed to be perfect for but instead has destroyed.

Finally, the Big Idea genre, Coyne says, synthesizes all three of the nonfiction categories. The Big Idea blends Narrative Nonfiction into How-To steps with Academic thoroughness that hooks an audience, proves a thesis, and leaves them with some actionable process for personal or social change.[5] Similar to the way atmospherics blends all other five domains in the study of situational awareness, the Big Idea form wraps the others together but also stands on its own.

The advantage of a Big Idea work is that it is usually . . . well, big. By satisfying all three types of genre requirements, the Big Idea drives some type of structural change that extends beyond the intended original audience. The challenge with chasing the Big Idea is that it is difficult to pull off. Big Ideas are often stumbled on rather than deliberately pursued.

An example in American nonfiction is George Kennan's 1946 "long telegram" and subsequent *Foreign Affairs* article. Written under the pseudonym X, Kennan, then the US deputy chief of mission to the Soviet Union, dispatched a lengthy essay back to Washington in response to a policy query, arguing against withdrawing all US military forces from Europe and advocating a "containment" strategy. Although his audience was primarily from the Academic genre—technical and specialized in the language of politics, government, and strategy—Kennan's Big Idea resonated well beyond the actual recipients. Following his death in 2005 at age 101, the *New York Times* described Kennan as "the American diplomat who did more than any other envoy of his generation to shape United States policy during the Cold War."[6]

Story Elements + Genre Classification = Field Research Presentation

This brings us back to Aristotle. The Big Idea genre is the only nonfiction form that demands a full balance of ethos, pathos, and logos to be complete. With the other three genres, one element is more important than the other two, and these become supporting elements for that particular genre's primary focus.

Think about this for a moment. Academic material must have logos because advancing an academic argument requires rational proof and factual analysis. How-To presentations depend on ethos because if the speaker is not seen as credible, the audience has no interest in listening to his or her advice. Narrative Nonfiction must have pathos because without an established emotional connection, the narrative feels empty, falls flat, and fails to advance the subject matter's theme and controlling idea.

This technique of genre classification is essential as we decide how best to present our material. Perhaps you are an academic, but your audience is really expecting instructional guidance or narrative entertainment. You might be a corporate researcher, but the boss is looking for technical data to have emerged from your fieldwork. And government researchers, while often generating seemingly dull after-action reports following a fact-finding visit, also confront the dilemma of being asked for their policy recommendation—in other words, their Big Idea—when presenting their executive summary or conclusions.

As a field researcher, you must know which genre you are working with and then identify the essential elements of other genres present in your material. If you are a journalist, look for patterns in your fieldwork that advance technical credibility or deepen an academic argument. If your field research is supposed to deliver practical results, search for the emotional and logical threads. If you are traveling to collect academic data, examine both the utility of what you have learned and the emotional resonance that extends to other comparable experiences.

Going back to our scenario, if you went to Lahore to research the philological differences between Urdu and Punjabi, your report will clearly be in the Academic genre. But perhaps part of those philology origins will have involved interesting and little-known religious rituals, which may have similarities to more common activities. Perhaps you met someone who reminded you of a loved one, and you could weave that Narrative Nonfiction emotion through your material. Or perhaps you observed a ritual that contributed to public health, and a How-To description would be an interesting addition to your report.

Conversely, if the reason you were in Lahore was for a cultural exchange, the audience attending a lecture on your experiences is probably expecting a Narrative Nonfiction presentation that covers a story arc of how your time in Pakistan changed your perspective on . . . everything. They want to feel your uncertainty; understand your expectations going in; be pulled through the bazaars, tea shops, sumptuous meals, religious conflicts, and political intrigues; and then walk away with some sense of how you felt about it all. Telling what you did and how you did it, using logos and ethos, brings a comfortable structure back into all that emotion. When your story works, you give the audience the basics, but do so with a twist.

Winning the Crowd

To win the crowd, as the character Maximus said in the movie *Gladiator*, you must give them something they have never seen before. This works only when you have already fulfilled the basic requirements inherent to the genre that your audience is expecting. Maximus, a general-turned-gladiator, knew the masses in the Coliseum wanted to see victory and defeat in mortal combat. He delivered that. What surprised the multitude was when the gladiator defied the emperor's order to kill a defeated opponent. The crowd, as depicted in the film, had never seen such an unexpected act of rebellion, yet it was fully authentic within the context.

For field researchers to win, they must first master the conventions of the genre their crowd anticipates from them. Once you understand the basic genre in which your likely audience is awaiting your material—Academic, How-To, or Narrative Nonfiction—you can move on to the convention you will use for the presentation. Most field researchers—especially starting out—should avoid going after the Big Idea genre in their presentations, reports, or essays.

Why is this? Because Big Idea material usually takes years of disciplined labor in one or more of the other nonfiction genres before it emerges on its own. For this reason, the Big Idea genre is important to understand but not healthy to initially pursue. If you have balanced logos, pathos, and ethos in your work, it is possible for a Big Idea to materialize. But those who pull it off—Thomas Friedman (*The World Is Flat*), Margaret Mead (*Coming of Age in Samoa*), Bruce Lee (*Tao of Jeet Kune Do*)—have typically toiled for years in a Narrative Nonfiction, Academic, or How-To genre before breaking through with a Big Idea.

Avoiding Death by PowerPoint

The first time you communicate your field data to someone else, you will generally do so in one of three ways: an in-person lecture, conversation, or discussion with an audience; an audio interview, recording, or podcast; or a written report, article, or essay. Each of these conventions has certain forms that are important to understand and respect. Since audio interviews, recordings, and podcasts are rarely the initial delivery requirement when returning from the field, we will focus on the two most common presentation methods: in person and in writing.

In-person lectures, conversations, and discussions usually rely on two things to generate audience interest: speaking ability and accompanying visuals. But the relationship between these variables has changed in the past two decades. Back in the twentieth century, if a speaker wanted a visual aid to accompany a presentation, the basic method was to use transparent plastic slides and manually change them on an overhead projector. The hassle of all this hardware often caused speakers to forego the visuals and instead emphasize their lectures.

Then PowerPoint changed everything. Following the software tool's ubiquitous ascent, the focus became the slide deck. But instead of being a positive enabling tool, PowerPoint presentations often made a poorly organized lecture even worse by more clearly exposing the speaker's muddled thinking. With technology and laptops enabling anyone to make a presentation, speakers began spending more time mastering their effects, graphs, charts, pictures, bullets, subheadings, and clip art than their presentation material. As General James Mattis bluntly told his staff after banning the tool's usage, "PowerPoint makes us stupid."[7]

Of course, PowerPoint itself isn't the problem. But using PowerPoint as a crutch has become so common that the first question a presenter should ask is, Do I really need slides at all? Slides should be used only for material that needs to be seen and not heard. Maps, charts, graphs, and photos are often important to your explanations—but a dozen more slides with extra bullets that restate your lecture are not. Your audience needs to hear what you are saying, not reread it again.

Seth Godin, entrepreneur and social change agent, offers these five rules for slide usage in his 2001 ebook *Fix Your Really Bad PowerPoint*:[8]

1. No more than six words on a slide. EVER.
2. No cheesy images. Use professional images. They cost $3 each or less; sometimes more if they're for "professional use."
3. No dissolves, spins or other transitions. None.
4. Sound effects can be used a few times per presentation, but never (ever) use the sound effects that are built in to the program. Instead, rip sounds and music from CDs and leverage the Proustian effect this can have.

5. Don't hand out print-outs of your slides. They're emotional, and they won't work without you there. If someone wants your slides to show "the boss," tell them that the slides go if you go.

So how do you weave slides like this into a compelling presentation? Most advice givers on presentations, including Seth Godin, tell speakers to match the slides with cue cards or note cards that follow a presentation script. This maintains a prepared flow while keeping your slide material fresh.

Patricia Ryan Madson, author of *Improv Wisdom*, takes this approach one step further. Instead of just writing statements on the cards, Madson encourages speakers to organize a list of questions about material ahead of time and answer them casually during a presentation.[9]

For example, this is how a statement might be written on your slide notecard:

Karahi gosht, a tomato-based mutton dish, is a specialty cuisine in Lahore, and families compete with each other for the best recipes.

What if you changed your note card to a question instead of a statement and then answered your question when giving your lecture? By writing the question instead of the statement, you will deliver a spontaneous answer to your audience that comes less from memorizing your script and more from the authenticity of your actual experience.[10] As a presenter, you will deliver an answer that is both prepared and spontaneous, the best of both worlds.

Phrased in a question form, your note card would read like this:

What is Lahore's specialty cuisine? How did I see it treated among friends and families during my time in the city?

When you write a question as a preemptive presentation cue instead of a statement, it means you don't have to stick completely to the script. Having the question prepared will give you confidence with where you're going with your material while also encouraging your audience to stay connected to you instead of their smartphones because your stuff feels fresh. Using Madson's method along with a select few maps, pictures, and/or statistics should suffice for presenting your material in person.

On Writing Well

If you are not asked to share your field research findings in person, then your work will most likely result in some initial written product for your client, sponsor, or boss. This might be anything from a formatted report to a journal article to a blog post. Regardless, submitting your material in writing has a different set of challenges and opportunities. In some ways, it is more difficult to narrate the story of your field data in print than in a presentation.

Dozens of manuals and guides have been written on English-language writing, and there's no need to restate that content here. But as mentioned in the presentation section, the first step for field researchers when writing material is to identify which genre readers will be anticipating. "When talented people write badly, it's generally for one of two reasons: either they're blinded by an idea they feel compelled to prove or they're driven by an emotion they must express," writes Robert McKee in his classic textbook *Story*. "When talented people write well, it is generally for this reason: they're moved by a desire to touch the audience."[11]

It might be difficult to think of "touching the audience" as an achievable goal when submitting an article for *Transactions of the American Philological Association* or filing a dispatch on what political corruption looks like in Peshawar or writing a guide on how to make *karahi gosht*. But moving them is exactly what you are intending to do, within the context of the genre your audience expects. Academic readers anticipate receiving information with your logos; Narrative Nonfiction readers will want your material to give them the subjective elements of pathos; How-To readers need proof of your ethos demonstrated in what you compose.

As with presentations, first identify the data you've collected that best matches the Aristotelian element most essential for your genre before writing anything. Then get that material in your document first. Know, understand, and respect your genre's conventions. Avoid writing narrative prose for an academic journal or filling a popular magazine article with arcane jargon. Consider adding pictures, step-by-step guides, or links to YouTube videos to accompany a how-to instruction piece. This will fulfill the initial requirement: deliver what the audience wants.

Once you've gotten the main stuff down, look for consistent themes that run through your piece and consider how you can bring in aspects of the remaining two elements of your genre in sentences, paragraphs, or transitions. Put another way, think of yourself as a screenwriter, and treat either logos, ethos, or pathos as your story's central plot and the remaining two elements as subplots. Screenwriters learn that a subplot may support, complicate, or contradict a central plot, which either expands an argument or illustrates a truth.[12]

More than anything, your audience, regardless of genre, demands you write the truth. And as we discussed in the previous chapter, they don't care as long as it is *your* truth—as long as you aren't faking it when you tell them what you learned in the field. Frauds in any genre are exposed, punished, and shunned. Deliver on the basics, and you will move your audience in the way they are expecting. As you do so, you will generate the potential to move them in an entirely unexpected way. Achieving this balance when sharing your data is what makes informing, enlightening, and entertaining possible.

Your field research material is only yours until you tell the story. This means it holds you captive until you present it either in person or on paper. After giving a presentation or submitting an article, you have let your discoveries go, and they will begin to take on a life of their own. In this respect, telling the story is the rite of passage you must endure before you will really be able to return home. As Proximo told Maximus on the eve of his first Coliseum duel, "Win the crowd, and you'll win your freedom."

Key Points

- The first principle to begin with for narrating your field experience is remembering that by assembling the data and information you collected in some type of arrangement, you are actually telling a story.
- Aristotle defined *ethos* (credibility), *pathos* (emotion), and *logos* (rational accuracy) as the elements that must exist for material presented to connect with an audience.
- Whether it is in a presentation or on paper, nonfiction work can be categorized into four main genres: Academic, How-To, Narrative Nonfiction, and The Big Idea.
- Academic, How-To, and Narrative Nonfiction genres demand primary focus on one of Aristotle's essential story elements (logos, ethos, and pathos) and use the other two as subordinate elements. The Big Idea genre requires all three.
- Before composing a presentation, field researchers must know which genre they are working with and then identify the elements of other genres in their material.

- In-person lectures, conversations, and discussions rely on your ability as a speaker and the interest your accompanying visuals generate with your audience.

- If you use PowerPoint, your slides should only add value to what you're saying and not duplicate your words. Slides are for material that has to be seen and not heard.

- For a talk or lecture, instead of writing statements on note cards, organize a list of questions about your material that you will answer during the presentation. This creates both structure and spontaneity in your speaking ability.

- Before preparing a report, article, or blog post from your field research, identify the material you've collected that matches the Aristotelian element most essential for your genre. Get that data in your document first.

- More than anything, your audience demands you write the truth. Deliver on the basics, and you will move them in the way they are expecting. In so doing, you will have the opportunity to inform, enlighten, and entertain them in new and unexpected ways.

Notes

1. Aristotle, *On Rhetoric: A Theory of Civic Discourse*, trans. George Kennedy (New York: Oxford University Press, 2006).

2. Shawn Coyne, "Nonfiction's Big Genre Silos," *The Story Grid* (blog), April 21, 2015, accessed September 5, 2015, www.storygrid.com.

3. Ibid.

4. Ibid.

5. Ibid.

6. "George F. Kennan Dies at 101; Leading Strategist of Cold War," *The New York Times*, March 18, 2005.

7. Elisabeth Blumiller, "'We Have Met the Enemy, and He Is PowerPoint,'" *The New York Times*, April 26, 2010, http://www.nytimes.com/2010/04/27/world/27powerpoint.html?_r=0.

8. Seth Godin, *Fix Your Really Bad PowerPoint*, 2001, accessed September 5, 2015, http://www.sethgodin.com/freeprize/reallybad-1.pdf.

9. Patricia Ryan Madson, *Improv Wisdom: Don't Prepare, Just Show Up* (New York: Random House, 2005), 56–57.

10. Ibid.

11. Robert McKee, *Story: Substance, Structure, Style, and the Principles of Screenwriting* (New York: HarperCollins, 1997), 7.

12. Ibid., 227–29.

9

Coming Home

The assignment is finished. The report is delivered. The brief has been given. You have been there and done it.

Your client was impressed and paid you on time. The department chair attended your presentation, expressed pride in your efforts, and promised future collaboration. The program manager noted your exemplary report to the contracting officer, ensuring another year of funding for your research company.

You are no longer an aspiring neophyte but an experienced veteran.

You have come full circle.

Now what?

Coming home is a process that each field researcher will go through in a different way. The emotions that accompany returning from encountering the Other usually fall within the bell curve of extremes that define a field research experience. Sometimes, you simply feel perpetually agitated. You did what you needed to do in the field, but you don't feel comfortable back at home. You don't even know how to explain it to yourself.

On one end of the spectrum are returning fieldworkers who suffer miserable, debilitating, or traumatic events. These researchers have been counting the days until getting home and never intend to go back into the field again. On the other side of the curve are researchers who fall in love with life abroad. Their main goal often evolves from one field stage to another through a series of expatriate identities where home becomes wherever they lay their heads.

Whether you have dozens more assignments or no other projects for the rest of your life, the skills you have developed in the field have moved you mentally, emotionally, and spiritually like nothing else has. The field is not an abstraction anymore but a deeply meaningful place. And when you attempt to talk about your time out of the country with someone who has never traveled, you feel like an outcast.

In any case, the most complicated aspect of coming back is usually not identifying bias or telling the story. On the contrary, in both story and life, the most difficult moments of any journey are finding the path home. It's where you strive to make everything you've learned real, but you feel as though no one else understands. Regardless of which extreme you lean toward on the spectrum, the odds are you will feel something more complicated than what people say you are supposed to feel.

How does a field researcher handle a theoretical, hoped-for sense of completion that never seems to arrive? Do you keep taking one assignment after another, traveling and moving and never settling down? Or do you find a safe place where you can use your field experience for a long time, telling your stories and making your successful assignment personally and professionally meaningful? Do you have to choose between these two options? Can you do both?

It depends entirely on you. Once you have learned and accomplished the researcher's professional skills, you may find that you were born for this trade as a duck is to water. If so, then when you return, you will never quite be able to keep your feet in the same place for long. You will inevitably look for the next departure, the next initiation, the next cycle—not so much because you are restless but because your instinct to uncover research opportunities is as natural as a chef's desire to cook.

Most of this book has been instructional by design—a How-To genre guide for aspiring practitioners of the field researcher's craft. But offering homecoming guidance is a little different. There's no scripted recommendation I—or anyone—can provide for what your next steps should be in your journey through fieldwork. "To make an end is to make a beginning," wrote T. S. Eliot. "The end is where we start from."

Perhaps a part of you has been awakened by exposure to the Other in ways you had not previously imagined. You may not feel fully at home there—wherever "there" is—but you feel as though you might not quite fit in here anymore either. Although you are not necessarily looking for the next gig, you have no ambition to pursue any professional endeavor that won't allow you, at some point, to return to the field.

Finding your path home, wherever home is, will inevitably involve deciding to what degree you wish to remain a member of this minority you have just discovered. Part of the way you find the answer to this question, and find your path, is from the stuff in you—the hardware that is organic to your brain, DNA, and soul. And part is the experiences that happen to you, both good and bad. This alchemy of genetics and environment gets processed through your being in a way that is as distinctive to you as a snowflake.

Which means part of your identity, if you've gone into the field—and if you keep going back out again and again and again—is that you will inevitably feel the duality of being at home everywhere and nowhere at once. No matter what passport you carry, a part of you can feel appreciated only for who you are in the land of investigative travelers. You feel fully at home in places you repeatedly learn, love, and leave.

It is probably too romantic, perhaps even unprofessional, for a field researcher to describe the enthusiasms of his or her work as something felt beyond the thrill many receive by traveling for any reason. But if you went into the field to research, you most likely did so while sensing a calling toward a place, event, or idea. By going to wherever you went, you inevitably became initiated into a small club of people from your circle who have worked, lived, and thrived in another place.

Then again, I have my own positionality just like everyone else. For whatever reason, I've felt a powerful draw for over a decade to the professional field researcher's life. And if you feel that same sense of calling as I have, I suspect you know it inside your bones and marrow because it is a calling—no different than medicine, or law, or the clergy, or education, or military service, or any other life dream. When you've done something that few can do—and done it well—why wouldn't you want to keep going forward on a fulfilling path?

In J. R. R. Tolkien's epic *The Lord of the Rings*, one of the central lines in a poem is "Not all those who wander are lost." The quote refers to the Rangers, a disparate group of vagabonds whom most of Middle-earth's population viewed with suspicion because of their rootlessness. It is this very wanderlust, however, that eventually enabled the group's leader, Aragorn, to forecast the coming dangers and inspire his followers to victory.

Embracing the life of the wanderer feels lonely at times. Living in the field and returning with firsthand insights from somewhere else is an unconventional vocation. But it certainly isn't impossible or unnecessary. Yes, we can access facts instantaneously through the internet. But those facts scream for context and depth in a way that the speed of technology slowly deters.

For me, this is what makes the field researcher's trade relevant to the general public—it is a profession that has both personal meaning and practical value. A field researcher brings insight back from lesser-known places, keeping the newness of discovery alive amid the illusion that we can have all the data we ever would need at our fingertips. In this small way, field researching take us closer to our shared humanity.

Perhaps your homecoming will be a permanent condition; you may have only one or two assignments before moving on to a stable routine. Or maybe you will be like one of Middle-earth's Rangers: a rootless, wandering vagabond for whom the mystery of worlds unseen, unknown, and undiscovered is not a siren song but a way of life. Or perhaps you will discover a balance between seasonal research and a base, limiting trips abroad to two or three client projects or breaks during the academic year.

Whether your field research career is a one-time experience or a lifetime profession, you will discover the right fit in your own way. One of the keys to coming home from any experience that brings you into a new world is not choosing between one or the other but comprehending how to be present in both, in some way, at the same time.

Although the laws of physics may say you cannot be in multiple places simultaneously, I have had a different experience amid my own mental, psychological, and emotional attempts to balance fieldwork with "normal" life. The more time I have spent in the field, the more worlds have become a part of me, and I of them. In so doing, I felt part of an invaluable and eccentric imagined community, a citizen of the nation of curious souls.

In this respect, no matter your profession, the thirsty inquisitiveness that field research slakes might remain both a blessing and a curse. Some of your colleagues and loved ones may admire you for being "adventurous" for going places they perceive as dangerous, even though to you the trips seem common. Your travels may be interpreted as careless or foolhardy, as an escape from the duties or responsibilities of a mortgage or 401(k). Your wanderings may be fully understood only by other researchers, by those who chronicle and analyze for, ultimately, no reason other than their own interest.

Sudhir Venkatesh certainly learned this. During his first days as a University of Chicago sociology student, he found himself attempting to collect data on gang members, traveling from those opposite worlds we discussed in chapter 1, using surveys asking, How does it feel to be black and poor? Discovering the emptiness in his questions without experiential context, Venkatesh spent months, then years, living with gangs and their families in Chicago's housing projects, work he later turned into his first of several best-selling books. Through his field research, Venkatesh went from being as out of place as a raincoat in the Sahara Desert to one of the most well-known sociologists in the world.

So, yes, if who you are involves traveling professionally, then you will find a way to be in two places at once. Your research might be part of a formal job with a large organization or as an independent contractor moving from one project to another. Along the way, you will make twists and turns, and the line will unfold in ways you wouldn't have known how to expect or predict when you started.

The ability to travel at will in the modern age is a mysterious and amazing phenomenon. A century ago, the only times most people went to new countries were as seafaring merchants, gilded tourists, or conscripted warriors. Today, global transportation systems provide the capacity to go anywhere, leaving border gatekeepers and governing authorities as the only barriers to entry. Through technology, we can transcend time and space in ways science can explain rationally but that remain no less magical in their reality.

In 1987, while dying of AIDS, writer Bruce Chatwin traveled to Australia to research his final book. *The Songlines*, published just before his death, describes his wanderings through the Outback with Aborigines. At the time he took the trip, Chatwin only knew he was sick—his malady had not yet been diagnosed—and that fueled a sense of urgency to travel and write the book. "His illness did him a favor," his friend Salman Rushdie said. "Otherwise, he would have gone on writing it for ten years."[1]

The aboriginal way of life, as Chatwin describes, is not linear and controlled by time. There is a relationship between land, souls, life, and song. Travels are not driven by season or weather or recreation or life event. Your travels are connected to the song you sing—the original expression of your life and dreams that takes form around a city or desert, state or mountain, world or ocean. This is the music you make. This is the story you tell. This is the song whose line you walk.

Ultimately, I am not a professional field researcher because of whatever value my trade brings to my clients or the public. My research may benefit people—I hope it does—but the reason I do it is because I love this line of work. For me, and perhaps other professional researchers, many of my deepest and most meaningful life experiences feel intimately connected with airport terminals, train stations, and bus rides. These have been my songlines of discovery, voyages that have taken me into places and ideas and realms I did not know were real until I found they were.

My life as a field researcher has involved learning how to observe, note, and narrate. It has required an ability to understand danger and transcend risk by paying attention and choosing as well as I could. It has demanded moving beyond fear that restricts while retaining awareness of caution that guides.

But most of all, field research has permanently made the Other a part of me. Each new place has humbled me as I witnessed the breadth and depth of human experience. Each new culture has taught me how similar and diverse we all really are. Each new presentation has shown me the power of logic, belief, and emotion when shared in a story.

For field researchers, I think that is, in the end, why we apply for grants or seek client projects or analyze new market opportunities. Researching is both what we do and who we are. We are looking for something we know is out there left to find, journeying through songlines as deeply personal as anything else we discover in our short lives. Regardless of however much time we spend in the field, our journey takes us one small step closer toward that giant leap of finding ourselves.

Safe travels, my friends, wherever you go.

I look forward to seeing you in the field.

Key Points

- If you went into the field as a researcher, you may struggle to explain the feeling of a calling you have experienced toward a place, event, or idea to those who have not been there. In both story and life, the hardest part of any journey is often finding the path back home.
- The key to coming home and living as a professional field researcher is not choosing between home and the field but comprehending how to live within both worlds at the same time.
- Most of all, field research has, at some level, permanently made what was once the Other a part of the researcher's life experience.

Note

1.   Nicholas Shakespeare, *Bruce Chatwin* (New York: Viking, 1999), 450.

Finishing Touches
Review Questions

Chapter 7: Objectivity Is a Myth

- Does field research bring a rare form of expertise to professionals who practice its art and science? What effect can this expertise have on field researchers after they have completed their fieldwork?
- What types of questions must you ask and answer as a field researcher before starting to build out the story of your fieldwork?
- How do biases change after completing a field research assignment? Why is this important to acknowledge up front?
- Why is it important to look for the gaps in your data? Is acknowledging the information that is not in your material up front likely to strengthen or weaken the quality and credibility of your work? Explain.
- Is awareness of the limitations in your research data likely to delegitimize your research or enhance your capacity to communicate what you did see? Explain.
- What one intangible feeling, above all else, should the opportunity to practice the art and science of field research inspire within those who call it their profession?

Chapter 8: Telling the Story

- Why is it important when narrating your field experience to remember that you are telling a story?
- What three core elements of a story did Aristotle identify in *On Rhetoric*? Why are these important to know?
- What are the four genres nonfiction work can be categorized into? How do these relate to Aristotle's three core story elements?
- Is it important to know which nonfiction genre convention you are working with before presenting your material? Why or why not?

- How should you use PowerPoint when giving an in-person presentation? What should the relationship be between your slides and your lecture?
- For a talk or lecture, what is another tool you can use instead of writing statements on note cards to add freshness and spontaneity to your material?
- When preparing a report, article, or blog post from your field research, what type of field data is most essential to get into your document first?

Chapter 9: Coming Home

- What is often the most difficult part of coming back home? Why?
- What is one way to describe the key to coming home and living as a professional? Would you describe this as a spiritual process? Why or why not?
- Have you had any similar experiences in relating to the Other as the handbook describes? How have they affected you, both professionally and personally?

Appendix A

Sample Research Proposal and Travel Budget

Field Research Proposal Template

Name of organization and/or prospective client:
[The proposal recipient]

Name of field researcher:
[You or your organization]

Name of proposed project:
[Title should include proposed research region]

Project time frame:
[Total weeks/months required, inclusive of field research and presentation]

Issue statement:
[Concise statement, perhaps one or two pages at most, of the corporate, academic, or public policy issue your proposed project will address. Include in your statement what you perceive the overall impact, or "value add," of your field research will be on the issue.]

Project personnel:
[You and anyone else]

Methods/Analytical approach:
[Expanded description of the issue, your field research intentions, and proposed approach]

Products:
[What you will deliver—i.e., report, presentation, etc.]

Field Research Budget Template

Research Trip #1 [xx days or weeks] _____
Flight _____
Ground Transportation _____
Lodging _____
Meals _____
Internet _____
Incidental Expenses _____

Research Trip #2 [xx days or weeks] _____
Flight _____
Ground Transportation _____
Lodging _____
Meals _____
Internet _____
Incidental Expenses _____
Honorariums [as required] _____

TOTAL BUDGET _____

Appendix B
Field Research Itinerary Sample Template

Itinerary: Silk Road Research
Uzbekistan, Kyrgyzstan, Tajikistan, Kazakhstan

April 13–14	Travel from USA to Tashkent, Uzbekistan
	[Flight itinerary and numbers]
April 14	Arrive in Tashkent, Uzbekistan
	Stay at [Hotel]
April 15	1500: Meet with journalist, politician, author
	[contact information]
	Stay at [Hotel or Airbnb?]
April 16	1000: Meet with deputy director, national security
	[contact information]
	Stay at [Hotel or Airbnb?]
April 17	Bus from Tashkent, Uzbekistan, to Shymkent, Kazakhstan
	Observations and informal interviews
	Stay at [Hotel or Airbnb?]
April 18	Shymkent
	Observations and informal interviews
	Stay at [Hotel or Airbnb?]
April 19	Bus from Shymkent, Kazakhstan, to Taraz, Kazakhstan
	Observations and informal interviews
	Stay at [Hotel]
April 20	Taraz
	1600: Interview, director of Centre for American Studies
	Background/contact information
	Stay at [Hotel]
April 21	Bus from Taraz, Kazakhstan, to Merki, Kazakhstan
	Observations and informal interviews
	Meet with host family from Workaway.info
	Stay with host family

April 22–26	Merki, Kazakhstan
	Stay with host family
April 27	Bus from Merki, Kazakhstan, to Bishkek, Kyrgyzstan
	Observations and informal interviews
	Stay at [Airbnb]
April 28	1000: Coffee with Kyrgyz government contact
	Stay at [Airbnb]
April 29–30	Bishkek
	Meetings, as possible
	Observations and informal interviews
	Stay at [Airbnb]
May 1	Fly from Bishkek, Kyrgyzstan, to Dushanbe, Tajikistan
	Observations and informal interviews
	Stay at [Hotel]
May 2	Dushanbe, Tajikistan
	1700: Meet with Tajik cinematographer for drinks
	Observations and informal interviews
	Stay at [Hotel]
May 3–4	Dushanbe
	Meetings, as possible
	Observations and informal interviews
	Stay at [Hotel]
May 5	Bus from Dushanbe, Tajikistan, to Samarkand, Uzbekistan
	Observations and informal interviews
	Stay at [Airbnb]
May 6–7	Samarkand
	Meetings, as possible
	Observations and informal interviews
	Stay at [Airbnb]
May 8	Bus from Samarkand, Uzbekistan, to Tashkent, Uzbekistan
	Observations and informal interviews
	Stay at [Hotel]
May 9–10	Tashkent
	Meetings, as possible
	Observations and informal interviews
	Stay at [Hotel]
May 11	Travel from Tashkent, Uzbekistan, to USA
	[Flight itinerary and numbers]

Suggested Reading

Part I: Research Preparation

Becker, Elizabeth. *Overbooked: The Exploding Business of Travel and Tourism*. New York: Simon & Schuster, 2013.

de Becker, Gavin. *The Gift of Fear and Other Survival Signals that Protect Us from Violence*. New York: Random House, 1997.

Pease, Allan, and Barbara Pease. *The Definitive Book of Body Language*. London: Orion, 2004.

Van Horne, Patrick, and Jason A. Riley. *Left of Bang: How the Marine Corps' Combat Hunter Program Can Save Your Life*. New York: Black Irish Entertainment LLC, 2014.

Venkatesh, Sudhir. *Gang Leader for a Day: A Rogue Sociologist Takes to the Streets*. New York: Penguin, 2008.

Part II: The Field

Dahlby, Tracy. *Into the Field: A Foreign Correspondent's Notebook*. Austin: University of Texas Press, 2014.

Diener, Alexander C., and Joshua Hagen. *Borders: A Very Short Introduction*. New York: Oxford University Press, 2012.

Franz, Carl, and Lorena Havens. *The People's Guide to Mexico*. Emeryville: Avalon, 1972.

Hasbrouck, Edward. *The Practical Nomad: How to Travel around the World*. Emeryville: Avalon, 2011.

Lewis, Benny. *Fluent in 3 Months: How Anyone at Any Age Can Learn to Speak Any Language from Anywhere in the World*. New York: HarperCollins, 2014.

Part III: Finishing Touches

Chatwin, Bruce. *The Songlines*. New York: Penguin Books, 1988.

Godin, Seth. *Fix Your Really Bad PowerPoint*. Ebook, sethgodin.com, 2001.

Madson, Patricia Ryan. *Improv Wisdom: Don't Prepare, Just Show Up*. New York: Random House, 2005.

McKee, Robert. *Story: Substance, Structure, Style, and the Principles of Screenwriting*. New York: HarperCollins, 1997.

Source Notes

PART I. Research Preparation

1. Framing the "Other"

Statistics on tourism come from chapter 1 of Elizabeth Becker's *Overbooked: The Exploding Business of Travel and Tourism*. Harry F. Wolcott's *The Art of Fieldwork* is focused on ethnography, but the principles and discussion apply across the spectrum of academic, corporate, and government field research. Jakub Grygiel's "Educating for National Security" (*Orbis*: Spring 2013) discusses the importance of travel in shaping national security policy and argues this is an art as much as, or more than, a science.

George Friedman's quotes on exploration come from a November 2010 Stratfor article, "The Geopolitical Traveler." BAMCIS, the acronym referencing the six troop-leading steps in the Marine Corps, stands for Begin planning, Arrange reconnaissance and coordination, Make reconnaissance, Complete the plan, Issue the order, Supervise. Sudhir Venkatesh's quote is from *Gang Leader for a Day*'s first chapter: "How Does it Feel to Be Black and Poor?"

Horace Mitchell Miner's "Body Ritual Among the Nacirema" debuted in the June 1956 issue of *American Anthropology* and has been making the rounds in college classrooms ever since. Philosophers credit Friedrich Hegel as among the first to define "the Other" as present in self-consciousness, dating back to the early nineteenth century.

2. Developing Your Research Style

Christopher Ingraham's *Washington Post* blog entry on Red Lake County and article on his subsequent visit were among the site's most-read articles in August and September 2015. Margaret Mead has been written about at length, and the works cited are only a nod to her lasting influence on the ideas associated with field research.

The typology and categorization of academic, corporate, and government research is my own. Michael Perry's guidance on how to look at a
small town comes from the paperback edition of *Population: 485*, his book
about working at a volunteer fire department in rural Wisconsin.

3. Improving Situational Awareness

Situational awareness is a complex topic, and *Left of Bang*, as credited in
the text, is an exceptionally useful primer for any researcher of any field.
The six domains as listed were originally developed for combat opera-
tions; Van Horne and Riley have distilled them into more practical, if still
technical, language for civilians, and I gratefully credit them with developing and publishing the template I narrated. This entire book is well
worth reading as a primer on situational awareness for anyone, anywhere.

Statistics on speech development and nonverbal communication come
from Allan and Barbara Pease's *The Definitive Book of Body Language*, which
also served as one of several resources for the general discussion. Others
included Joe Navarro's *What Every BODY Is Saying*; Houston, Floyd, and
Carnicero's *Spy the Lie: Former CIA Officers Teach You How to Detect Deception*; and Nierenberg and Calero's *How to Read a Person Like a Book*. John
Baldoni's Forbes.com article "7 Surprising Truths about Body Language"
was a helpful reminder of the limitations.

For the field anecdotes referenced, I traveled to the Baltics in April
2015 and to Senegal, Niger, and Mali in March/April 2013.

PART II. The Field

4. Logistics and Networking

Planning for field time is a highly personal process. Observations,
thoughts, and anecdotes on logistics planning and networking preparation are drawn substantially from my own field research experience
and anecdotal conversations with other professional field researchers—particularly those of different backgrounds and experiences. I
cross-referenced recommendations with Edward Hasbrouck's *The Practical Nomad*, Robert Young Pelton's *The World's Most Dangerous Places*,
Andrew Mueller's *I Wouldn't Start from Here*, and Carl Franz and Lorena
Havens's *The People's Guide to Mexico*.

Beyond the websites mentioned in the text, Chris Guillebeau's blog,
"The Art of Non-Conformity," is well worth a field researcher's review.
Guillebeau has visited every country in the world and succeeded in upset-

ting just about everyone's apple cart for reconsidering the value of travel, entrepreneurship, and how just about anyone can make a living doing whatever they want.

5. On the Ground

In several cases, the explanatory sections of the chapter specified the observation and context of the research. At other times, I have deliberately left the circumstances more ambiguous by virtue of my own existing nondisclosure agreements as a field researcher.

Benny Lewis is an Irish polyglot who developed the website fluentinthreemonths.com and wrote the book with the same title. Widely known for a TED talk featuring his language-learning approach, Benny was (as of 2015) fluent in eleven languages. His advice is practical, effective, and can easily be applied even if you don't have time to read the book.

My thoughts and recommendations on "cover" are also derived from my own field experiences.

6. The Interview

The fictitious scenario used as a case study in this chapter was amalgamated from several dozen field interviews I completed during my time spent as a contract researcher for the US State Department Bureau of Diplomatic Security's Antiterrorism Assistance Program. The interview descriptions were compiled from the publicly available Qualitative Research Guidelines Project, which, in turn, compiled the standards from qualitative research textbooks.

In over a decade of freelance writing and field research, I have completed several hundred interviews and been interviewed myself dozens of times. I have derived the template and recommendations from reflecting on my own experiences as well as from conversations with anthropologists, field agents, and professional journalists. Credit for the interview conclusion recommendation goes to David Halberstam, who, according to Robert Timberg, claimed that he always ended every interview by asking who else he should talk to.

PART III. Finishing Touches
7. Objectivity Is a Myth

As with the rest of this book's content, this chapter's purpose is to move beyond the existential, academic, and theoretical arguments. The goal of highlighting this experience as a field researcher is not to discuss whether or not objective truth is achievable but rather to acknowledge the challenge field researchers face with objectively presenting their experience in any form. Narrations and presentations may be factually accurate while also substantively incomplete. As the chapter emphasizes, a sense of humility is of paramount importance when sifting through the mass of data and notes collected during field research.

Wallace Stevens's quote at the beginning of the chapter is from the first stanza of his poem "Metaphors of a Magnifico" and is in the public commons. Lane Wallace wrote about the myth of objectivity in a July 2009 essay in *The Atlantic* that illustrated why the US Supreme Court would benefit from Justice Sonia Sotomayor's addition to the bench. Richard Taflinger's "The Myth of Objectivity in Journalism: A Commentary" was published in May 1996 on the Washington State University website and is a helpful primer on the reporter's eternal challenge.

Arjun Appadurai's "Grassroots Globalization and the Research Imagination" adds scholarly heft toward the call to understand each layer of bias we struggle with as researchers. I quoted my FPRI colleague Walter McDougall's February 1998 essay "The Three Reasons We Teach History," a piece whose thesis reinforced to me the importance of treating any research pursuit with a sense of unpretentiousness and modesty.

8. Telling the Story

Aristotle's three elements of story from *On Rhetoric* have clearly stood the test of time, as has some of his other Big Idea material. I cross-referenced the George Kennedy translation with several online sites discussing his work.

Shawn Coyne's four genres of nonfiction come from his excellent blog, www.storygrid.com. Coyne had originally framed the nonfiction genre categories only through examining written material—mostly books and other narrative articles—and I expanded it to include lectures and presentations for the field researcher's benefit. The genre interpretations, as a field researcher should employ them for sorting material, reflect my own personal take on Coyne's work.

Seth Godin's "Fix Your Really Bad PowerPoint" ebook, from which I pillaged, should be mandatory reading in classrooms, cubicles, and conference rooms worldwide. Patricia Ryan Madson's *Improv Wisdom* is a great read not only for lectures but for anyone seeking to develop a sense of spontaneity toward life in general.

9. Coming Home

As with other chapters, many of the thoughts expressed are my own. Some of the ideas in this section were developed from my previous book on how American combat veterans transition into civilian life, *The Return: A Field Manual for Life After Combat*, in addition to reflecting on my own transitions and choices.

Over the years, J. R. R. Tolkien's second line of a poem repeated twice in *The Lord of the Rings* has often reminded me of my own profession's value. And Bruce Chatwin's *The Songlines* takes homecoming and field research into a category all its own.

Selected Bibliography

Aristotle. *On Rhetoric: A Theory of Civic Discourse*. Translated by George Kennedy. New York: Oxford University Press, 2006.

Becker, Elizabeth. *Overbooked: The Exploding Business of Travel and Tourism*. New York: Simon & Schuster, 2013.

Campbell, Joseph. *The Hero with a Thousand Faces*. New York: Pantheon Books, 1949.

Chatwin, Bruce. *The Songlines*. New York: Penguin Books, 1988.

Coyne, Shawn. *The Story Grid: What Good Editors Know*. New York: Black Irish Entertainment LLC, 2015.

Dahlby, Tracy. *Into the Field: A Foreign Correspondent's Notebook*. Austin: University of Texas Press, 2014.

Danelo, David J. *The Return: A Field Manual for Life after Combat*. New York: Black Irish Entertainment LLC, 2014.

de Becker, Gavin. *The Gift of Fear and Other Survival Signals that Protect Us from Violence*. New York: Random House, 1997.

Diener, Alexander C., and Joshua Hagen. *Borders: A Very Short Introduction*. New York: Oxford University Press, 2012.

Franz, Carl, and Lorena Havens. *The People's Guide to Mexico*. Emeryville: Avalon, 1972.

Godin, Seth. *Fix Your Really Bad PowerPoint*. Ebook, sethgodin.com, 2001.

Hasbrouck, Edward. *The Practical Nomad: How to Travel around the World*. Emeryville: Avalon, 2011.

Houston, Philip, Michael Floyd, Susan Carnicero, and Don Tennant. *Spy the Lie: Former CIA Officers Teach You How to Detect Deception*. New York: St. Martin's Press, 2012.

Lewis, Benny. *Fluent in 3 Months: How Anyone at Any Age Can Learn to Speak Any Language from Anywhere in the World*. New York: HarperCollins, 2014.

Lloyd, Martin. *The Passport: The History of Man's Most Travelled Document*. England: Sutton Publishing Limited, 2003.

Madson, Patricia Ryan. *Improv Wisdom: Don't Prepare, Just Show Up*. New York: Random House, 2005.

Markus, Hazel Rose, and Alana Conner. *Clash! How to Thrive in a Multicultural World*. New York: Plume, 2013.

McKee, Robert. *Story: Substance, Structure, Style, and the Principles of Screenwriting*. New York: HarperCollins, 1997.

Miller, Rory. *Meditations on Violence: A Comparison of Martial Arts Training & Real World Violence*. Boston: YMAA Publication Center, 2008.

Miller, Rory. *Facing Violence: Preparing for the Unexpected*. Boston: YMAA Publication Center, 2011.

Mueller, Andrew. *I Wouldn't Start from Here: The 21st Century and Where It All Went Wrong*. Australia: Pan Macmillan, 2007.

Navarro, Joe. *What Every BODY Is Saying*. New York: HarperCollins, 2008.

Nierenberg, Gerard I., and Henry H. Calero. *How to Read a Person Like a Book*. New York: Barnes & Noble Books, 1994.

Nordstrom, Carolyn, and Antonius C. G. M. Robben. *Fieldwork under Fire: Contemporary Studies of Violence and Survival*. Berkeley: University of California Press, 1995.

Pease, Allan, and Barbara Pease. *The Definitive Book of Body Language*. London: Orion, 2004.

Pelton, Robert Young. *The World's Most Dangerous Places*. New York: Tembo LLC, 2003.

Perry, Michael. *Population: 485; Meeting Your Neighbors One Siren at a Time*. New York: Harper Perennial, 2007.

Pressfield, Steven. *The War of Art*. New York: Warner Books, 2002.

Stiffman, Arlene Rubin, ed. *The Field Research Survival Guide*. New York: Oxford University Press, 2009.

Van Horne, Patrick, and Jason A. Riley. *Left of Bang: How the Marine Corps' Combat Hunter Program Can Save Your Life*. New York: Black Irish Entertainment LLC, 2014.

Venkatesh, Sudhir. *Gang Leader for a Day: A Rogue Sociologist Takes to the Streets*. New York: Penguin, 2008.

Wolcott, Harry F. *The Art of Fieldwork*. Lanham: AltaMira Press, 2005.

Yin, Robert K. *Case Study Research: Design and Methods*. Thousand Oaks: SAGE Publications Inc., 2009.

Index

About the Author

David J. Danelo is an adjunct professor with the University of Texas at El Paso's National Security Studies Institute and the Director of Field Research for the Foreign Policy Research Institute, the top-ranked think tank in the United States with an operating budget under $5 million. Danelo graduated from the US Naval Academy in 1998 and served seven years as an infantry officer in the Marine Corps, including a 2004 combat tour in Iraq. Since leaving active duty, he has served as a senior US government policy executive, written about international affairs, and conducted field research in over fifty countries. He teaches a holistic, skills-based approach to field research, consults on international border management, and operates the Return Retreat, a nationally acclaimed program where combat veterans can navigate their transition and growth in a rugged, familiar environment. Danelo is the author of three previous books: *Blood Stripes: The Grunt's View of the War in Iraq*; *The Border: Exploring the U.S.-Mexican Divide*; and *The Return: A Field Manual for Life after Combat*. He is based in Philadelphia and West Texas.